PRESENTS

Fabulous Country-style Quilts

Craftworld Books

Contents

Home Sweet Home

Fabulous Country Style

TEXT BY KATE TULLY

What we refer to as 'country style' is not so much a mode of decorating as a way of life. Country style is not a look that one pays an interior decorator to produce. It is the result of an approach to life which delights in lavishing love and care on creating a comfortable home; a return to the much-maligned practice of homemaking.

Certainly, the country style represents what we now regard as old-fashioned values like security versus instability, gentleness versus harshness, serenity versus frenzy, and honesty versus pretence. But we enjoy the elements of country living today not just because they are wistful reminders of these values but because we are determined to inject these very values into our own lives. There are pleasures and

feelings of contentment known to our great grandparents which seem to have been lost for a few generations, and we are determined to rediscover them.

The term 'country' appears to encapsulate these pleasures and feelings for us. Perhaps not surprisingly, the country style of living is especially prized by those of us living in cities. As more and more of us are employed in service industries rather than in production, so we find that our daily routines provide little outlet for our creative urges.

And to create is certainly an irrepressible human urge. We love to see something tangible for our efforts. What better encouragement to create than the opportunity to 'create a home' – not just a house, but a place steeped in our own favourite colours, motifs, textures and objects through the work of our own hands?

The beauty of creating a home in the country style is that, by definition, this is a style for amateurs. While in all creative pursuits you can expect to improve with practice, it is possible to create a country ambience even as a complete novice.

Remember that most of the elements of country style that we so love, such as quilts, hail from the pre-industrial age. This was a time when ordinary people had neither the opportunity to buy items ready-made in stores, nor the funds to commission artisans to produce them, and relied instead on their own resourcefulness to fulfil their need for decorative comfort.

Craft items are often regarded merely as accessories. But with country crafts in particular, the homemaker's handiwork often forms the very framework of a room's appearance. Elements such as quilts, painted furniture and rugs are much more than accessories – they are essentials of the country-style home. Starting with quite basic elements, our creative forebears set to work to make them more attractive and individual.

One of the most common elements used has always been fabric. One of the most universally available and affordable fabrics over the last few hundred years has certainly been calico, the cheap cotton weave which is unbleached, undyed and can be used for every purpose from quilts to clothing. Calico was made more decorative by stencilling, dyeing and by using it in combination with more colourful fabrics in patchwork.

Any other fabrics available to earlier generations were used sparingly and resourcefully. Old blankets were made into coats and vice versa. Clothing, linen and any fabric which had passed its original usefulness was recycled into quilts, rag rugs or mattress filling. Decorative trims such as ribbon, braid and lace were carefully reused over and over again.

Indeed, there are two qualities which go hand-in-hand with the country style: resourcefulness and functionalism. Neither materials nor time were wasted on items which served only a decorative purpose. Quilts were certainly decorative but their primary function was to keep the family warm.

Early American settlers often had only the most rudimentary creative skills and even less money, so their homes were relatively primitive with scrap quilts, hand-hewn furniture and rag rugs. Distinctive styles such as the Amish with their beautiful quilts and the Shakers with their simple but elegant furniture are enjoying a renaissance. The predominant colours of these styles are timber tones and unbleached calico, with small touches of subdued blues, red, browns and greens.

The English countrywomen of the 19th century had rather more time to employ in the creation of their 'fancywork' and could afford more expensive materials. Their legacy is a more romantic variation of country style, characterised by embroidered tablecloths, muslin lavender sachets, white-on-white bedspreads with lace pillows and needlepoint firescreens.

Yet both have in common the reliance on basic skills learnt from the previous generation to make a home as comfortable as possible. The accessibility of their crafts is what we now find so attractive about the country style. ❆

Country Style

All quilts courtesy of Susanne Cody (02) 9969 1850.

Friendship Scrap Quilt

To make this colourful quilt, Virginia Edwards used all the 6in squares obtained from her sewing group's fabric exchanges. The challenge was to combine hundreds of designs and colours to produce harmony in her friendship quilt. This is also a way of using up fabric swatches.

PREPARATION

NOTE: Use either metric or imperial measurements throughout. You need a large assortment of light to medium-light and medium-dark to dark fabrics.

Wash and iron fabrics where possible – this may be difficult when using scraps and swatches. Cut out fabrics as indicated in the materials list – a quicker cutting method is to roller-cut 7.6cm (3in) strips of fabric and then cut these into 7.6cm (3in) squares. Similarly, cut 8.5cm (3⅜in) strips and cut these into 8.5cm (3⅜in) squares.

CONSTRUCTION

Note: Seam allowance is 6mm (¼in). The basis of this block, as you can see in the photograph, is the simple nine patch with the darker fabrics running across the middle and the lighter ones on the side.

Commence by joining the light and dark triangles (half squares) to form squares.

The squares are then sewn together in lines as per Diagram 1.

FIRST LINE:

1. Dark
2. Dark/light square
3. Light

SECOND LINE:

4. Light/dark square
5. Dark
6. Dark/light square

THIRD LINE:

7. Light square
8. Light/dark square
9. Dark square

The three rows of squares should then be pressed with seams facing outwards on the first line, in towards the centre on the second line and outwards again on the third line.

This enables the seams to be butted up to each other as the block is completed by sewing together the three rows of squares. As you complete each block, trim excess threads and make sure each block is approximately 20cm (8in) square.

ASSEMBLING THE QUILT TOP

Arrange the 80 blocks according to the quilt photograph on page 11 or as you desire. By manipulating your blocks many different designs can be achieved. In this case a trellis design was achieved.

In this quilt there are 10 rows, consisting of eight blocks each. When sewing, iron the seams in alternate directions. When you come to sew the rows together, the seam allowances will butt up against each other, matching the seams. Continue until all 10 rows are sewn together.

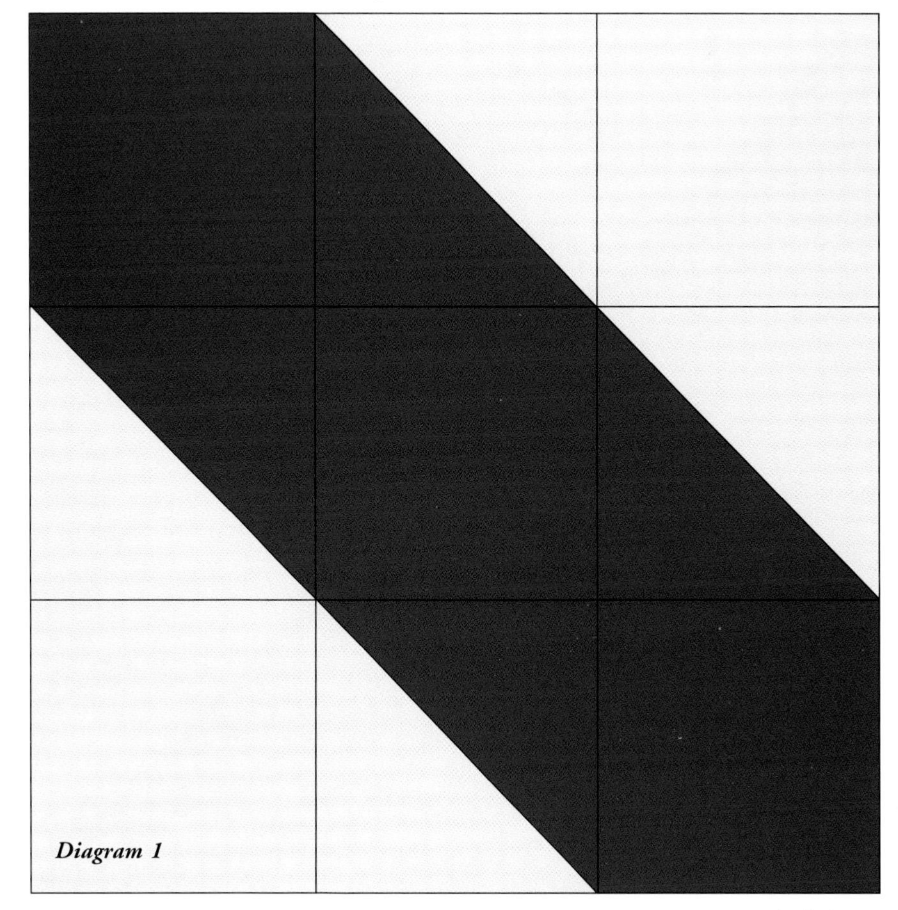

Diagram 1

FINISHED SIZE

- 148cm x 182cm (58in x 72in)

MATERIALS

- 240 x 7.6cm (3in) squares of assorted medium-dark and dark fabrics
- 160 x 7.6cm (3in) squares of assorted light and medium-light fabrics
- 160 x 8.5cm (3⅜in) squares of assorted medium-dark to dark fabrics, cut in half diagonally
- 160 x 8.5cm (3⅜in) squares of assorted light to medium-light fabrics, cut in half diagonally
- 2m (2¼yd) square of batting
- 3.3m x 115cm (3⅝yd x 45in) of backing fabric
- Rotary cutter, mat and ruler
- Matching machine thread
- Sewing machine and basic sewing supplies

QUILTING

Cut the backing fabric in half, removing all selvedges, and sew the pieces together along the longer side. Iron the seams open. Sandwich the backing, batting and quilt together, then pin and tack all three pieces together.

Virginia chose to have this particular quilt machine-quilted. If a quilt is to be machine-quilted, it does not have to be tacked as the three layers are brought together on the machine.

BINDING

From the backing fabric, cut 6.5cm (2.5in) strips. Join these until you have

enough binding to go around the quilt plus some extra – about 7m (7¾yd).

Press the binding in half with the wrong sides together and sew to the right sides of the quilt, matching the raw edges.

Fold the binding over the seam allowance to the back of the quilt, mitring the corners, and slip-stitch into place.

This quilt is the ideal project for using all those scraps sitting in your craft cupboard. ❆

Strawberry Picking with Grandad

Picking strawberries is a fun-filled pastime. Lynette Anderson's son, Edward, enjoyed picking strawberries with his grandfather so much that he drew a picture, which became the inspiration for this adorable quilt.

CENTRE BACKGROUND

From the five neutral prints and seeded cotton, cut nine, 5½in squares, nine, 3½in x 8½in rectangles and nine, 3½in x 5½in rectangles. Assemble the basic block, using a 6mm (¼in) seam allowance. Refer to the basic block diagram on the pattern sheet as a guide.

Make nine basic blocks. Join them to make three rows of three. Refer to the centre background diagram on the pattern sheet. Press the seams well.

BORDER

From the nine assorted fabrics and using the triangle template, cut 112 triangles with 6mm (¼in) seams using a random placement. Join the triangles to form a total of 28 squares.

Form two strips by joining six squares and press well. Join these strips to either side of the centre panel and press. For the top and bottom borders, form two strips by joining eight squares. Press well. Join top and bottom borders to the centre panel and press.

ADDING APPLIQUE PIECES

Trace the people, car, dog and ladybug appliqué shapes from the pattern sheet onto the paper side of the fusible webbing (the shapes have already been reversed). Cut out the shapes roughly, then iron the fusible webbing (paper side up) onto the wrong side of the appropriate fabrics. Use the photograph as a guide to the colours. Cut out each shape accurately and peel the backing paper from the fusible webbing. Check the photograph for positioning of the pieces and when they are in place, press with a hot iron. Using two strands of matching embroidery thread, Blanket-stitch around the edges of the appliqué shapes. Refer to the stitch diagram in the Stitch Guide on page 108.

Strawberry Leaves: Follow the initial steps for the fusible-webbing technique. However, when it comes to cutting out the leaves, use pinking shears instead of regular scissors. This gives a realistic look to the leaves.

Iron the leaves into position, then with two strands of embroidery thread and using a running stitch, outline the leaves and stitch the veins. Add a stalk in Stem Stitch. Place the stalk in the centre of the plant – these stems will be partially covered by ruched strawberry flowers.

Strawberries: Using the fusible-webbing appliqué technique, apply the strawberries cut from pink tones left over from the assorted fabrics.

Blanket-stitch around each strawberry shape with two strands of pink stranded cotton. Using two strands of dark green embroidery thread and one strand of light green, place some Lazy Daisy Stitches at the top of each strawberry. Vary the length of the stitches – this will look like the leaf at the top of the strawberry. Using Stem Stitch, add a stalk to each strawberry.

'PICK YOUR OWN' SIGN

Using one strand of ecru DMC cotton, Backstitch the writing on the board. Dots on the pattern indicate where to place the French Knots. You can either apply a strawberry onto the board using the fusible-webbing technique or stitch on a strawberry button.

FINISHED SIZE

- 80cm (32in) square

MATERIALS

- 20cm (¼yd) of five neutral prints (centre background)
- 20cm (¼yd) of nine assorted fabrics (appliqué and border)
- 10cm (⅛yd) seeded cotton
- 10cm (⅛yd) each of green, black, brown and navy
- 1m (⅛yd) backing fabric
- 1m (⅛yd) wadding
- 50cm (½yd) fusible webbing
- One strawberry and one hat button (optional)
- Two large buttons for hub caps
- Two small buttons
- 20cm (¼yd) narrow ribbon
- DMC Stranded Embroidery Cotton to match fabrics: dark green, light green, yellow, navy, blue, brown, black, pink and ecru
- DMC Coton Perlé No 5: ginger, grey, yellow
- Jo Sonja's Artists' Acrylics: Carbon Black, Titanium White, Burgundy
- Jo Sonja's Textile Medium
- Liner brush
- 2B pencil

STITCHES USED

Buttonhole Stitch, Lazy Daisy Stitch, Stem Stitch, French Knots, Satin Stitch, Colonial Knots, Couching

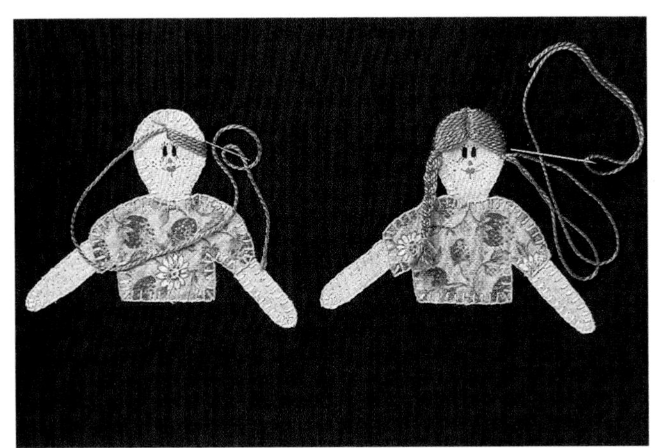

***Step 1** Using ginger DMC Coton Perlé No 5, fill in either side of the girl's part with Satin Stitch.*

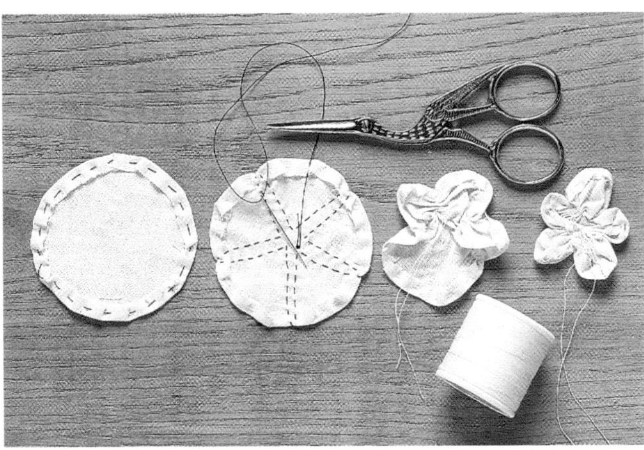

***Step 2** Gently, but firmly, pull on each end of the running thread to draw up the flower.*

CAR AND LADYBUG

To finish the car, sew two buttons in position on the wheels to act as hub caps. Use one strand of black stranded cotton to work the embroidery on the ladybug.

The eye is worked using a Lazy Daisy Stitch and is couched on either side of the stitch to hold the round shape.

The legs are embroidered using Backstitch and finished with Lazy Daisy Stitch feet.

The Ladybug's antennae are sewn in Backstitch and finished at each end with a French Knot.

BOY

Using ginger DMC Coton Perlé, Satin-stitch random lengths for the boy's hair. To finish the boy, sew two buttons onto his overalls. See the photograph for position.

GRANDAD'S HAIR

Using grey DMC Coton Perlé, sew a series of small loops and small safety stitches around the face and under the hat brim.

GIRL

With a 2B pencil, mark the centre part of the girl's hair. Using ginger DMC Perlé, fill in either side of the part with Satin Stitch. Take care not to pull the stitches too tightly or the head will pucker.

Following the Step 1 photograph, make three loops at B and C, cut the loops and plait with sewing cotton to hold and cover this with small ribbon bows. Finish the girl by sewing the hat button in her hand where it meets Grandad's.

FACES

Paint or embroider the faces. When painting on the fabric, you need to mix textile medium with the paint to prevent cracking. Follow the manufacturer's directions carefully.

The paint consistency needs to be fairly liquid, rather like milk – if it's too thick it will drag across your fabric, creating rough-looking edges; if you have it too runny, it will bleed into the warp and weft threads. You may like to practice first on a spare piece of calico.

RUCHED STRAWBERRY FLOWERS

From the seeded cotton, and using the template on the pattern sheet, cut 15 circles for the ruched flowers. Tack the seam allowance under using small running stitches, this row of tacking will be removed later. With a strong thread knotted at the end, stitch small running stitches, following the Step 2 photograph for stitch placement. Gently but firmly, pull on each end of the thread to draw up the flower. Pull tightly until you are satisfied with the shape of the flower. On the wrong side of the flower, tie the two ends of thread together and cut off the tails. Attach these flowers to the centre of your strawberry plants using blind stitch. Remove the row of tacking. With yellow DMC Coton Perlé, sew Colonial Knots in the centre of each flower to simulate stamens.

STRAWBERRY PLANTS

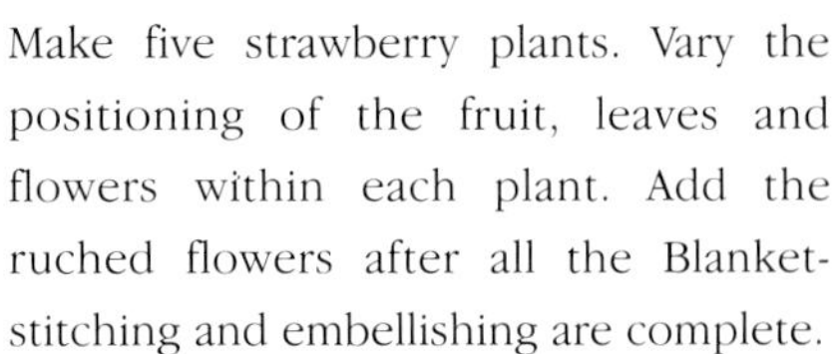

Make five strawberry plants. Vary the positioning of the fruit, leaves and flowers within each plant. Add the ruched flowers after all the Blanket-stitching and embellishing are complete.

LAYERING THE QUILT

Press the backing fabric and place on a flat surface, right side down. Next, place wadding on top of the backing, followed by the pressed quilt top (right side up), forming a sandwich. The backing and wadding should be about 5cm (2in) bigger than the quilt top.

Tack the three layers together using a medium-size running stitch. Tack in vertical and horizontal lines to form a grid spaced about 7.5cm-10cm (3in-4in) apart. Always sew your tacking from the centre outwards.

Now your quilt is ready for quilting. Stitch-in-the-ditch around all the shapes and use the strawberry and small leaf shapes as a template to fill in the larger areas.

BINDING

Cut a strip 1½in wide x the length of the four sides combined. This should be cut on the straight grain. Turn over one third of the binding along its entire length and press well. Then, with the quilt top facing you, place the unpressed edge of the binding on the edge of the quilt with right sides together.

Sew one side at a time, starting somewhere along the edge (not in a corner). Pin and machine-stitch to within

6mm (¼in) of the quilt top. Remove the quilt from the machine. Pin the next edge to be sewn into position. Remember to add a small fold of fabric at the corner to allow the binding to ease nicely around the bend. Repeat for all sides.

When you arrive back at the starting point, join the ends together before stitching the last edge.

Trim off any excess wadding and backing fabric. Turn the pressed edge of the binding to the back of the quilt and hand-stitch into place, covering the machine stitching.

Your quilt is now ready to hang in a special place in your home. ❄

Debonair Dining

Created by Susanne Cody, this delightful combination of embroidery, patchwork and quilting makes a splendid table runner. The runner can be enlarged by simply adding extra blocks or personalised by changing colours or stitching designs. Be as creative as you like!

PREPARATION

From the background fabric, tear 21, 5in squares (these will be trimmed to size later). Place each design from the pattern sheet onto the sandpaper board. Centre a 5in background square over the design and trace onto the fabric using the HB pencil. Repeat the butterflies and birds twice, varying details and stitches each time.

Note: These blocks are sewn into position 'on point' and it is essential that the arrow next to each design runs parallel to the grainline of the fabric.

From the background fabric, cut two each of Template 1 and 2. These are the pieces for the end of the table runner.

Trace the embroidery designs onto the fabric using the sandpaper board and a sharp HB pencil.

EMBROIDERY

Embroider the designs using the crewel needle and turkey red stranded cotton. Use two strands for larger details such as the leaves, stems and birds, and one thread for smaller details. Embroider 21 squares and the four triangular end pieces.

CUTTING

When the embroidery is completed, make a 3½in square template from the template plastic. Centre the template over the completed embroidery block on a cutting board and cut the block to the square using the rotary cutter. Repeat for all embroidered blocks.

From a variety of patchwork fabrics, cut 42, 3¼in squares. Cut each square in half diagonally using the rotary cutter. You will need a total of 84 triangles to complete this project. You can repeat colours, however Susanne's runner has a different fabric for each triangle.

Again, from the patchwork fabric, cut two each of Template 3, 4 and 5.

ASSEMBLY

Block Assembly: Add two triangles to opposite sides of an embroidered square. Then add another two triangles to the remaining sides. Use the photograph as a guide. Repeat for a total of 21 blocks.

When all the blocks have been assembled, join them together into three

FINISHED SIZE

- 108cm x 33cm (42½in x 13in)

MATERIALS

- 1m (1⅛yd) background fabric, a good quality homespun, calico or quilter's muslin
- 1.1m x 35cm (1¼yd x 13¾in) flannelette
- 1.1m x 35cm (1¼yd x 13¾in) backing fabric
- 20cm (¼yd) fabric for binding
- Variety of similar colour value patchwork fabrics
- DMC Stranded Embroidery Cotton: two skeins of turkey red (498)
- DMC Coton Perlé No 8: two balls of turkey red (498)
- No 10 crewel needle
- Quilting thread
- ¼in quilting tape
- Template plastic
- Cutting board, ruler and rotary cutter
- Sandpaper board
- Sharp HB pencil
- 90mm x 50mm (3½in x 13in) piece of thick cardboard

STITCHES USED

Stem Stitch, Backstitch, Running Stitch, Couching, French Knot, Outline Stitch

Using the sandpaper board, transfer each design onto centre of a 5in background square. It is essential that the arrow next to each design runs parallel to the fabric grainline.

Add two fabric triangles to the opposite sides of a 3½in embroidered background square. Then add another two fabric triangles to the remaining sides.

rows of seven blocks each and then sew the rows together.

End Assembly: Join embroidered Template 1 and 2 to either side of Template 3. Then join Template 4 to the other side of Template 1 and Template 5 to Template 2. Sew this section to the main body of the runner. Repeat the procedure for the other end of the runner.

BACKING

Lay the backing wrong side up on a table, place the flannelette over the backing and then place the runner right side up on top. Baste these three layers together.

QUILTING

Stitch-in-the-ditch around the edge of the embroidered squares and outline-stitch all embroidery. Use the quilting tape as a guide and quilt ever-decreasing squares and triangles in the patchwork squares and triangles. Susanne's shapes have decreased by ¼in each time.

BINDING

When the quilting is complete, trim away excess flannelette and backing. Cut the binding 1½in wide and press in half. Add the binding in two stages. Starting at a pointed end of the runner, machine-stitch the binding in place, tucking slightly at the corners and finishing at the other pointed end of the runner. Turn the binding over and slip-stitch in place. Repeat this process for the other side of the runner.

FINISHING

Wash the runner in hot water and dry using a hot cycle in your dryer to achieve shrinkage. This will give the runner an old-fashioned country look.

Make two tassels for the ends. Lie a 12in piece of red turkey Coton Perlé across the shorter side of a 3½in x 2in piece of cardboard 200 times. Using the 12in thread, pull the wraps together and knot securely, then cut the loops at the other end of the card to make the tassel skirt.

Take more thread and wrap tightly around the top section of the tassel, 1½in below the 12in thread. Complete about 20 wraps.

When complete, finish off the thread by burying it inside the tassel. Use the 12in thread to join the tassel to the end of the table runner.

Repeat the above steps to make the second tassel, joining it to the opposite end of the runner. ❄

ABCDE
IJKLM
RSTUV

Charming Country

All items courtesy of Primarily Patchwork (03) 9830 4537

A Thousand Pyramids

Designed and made by Janine Franzke for Primarily Patchwork, this charming and generous lap quilt uses a wealth of red, gold and blue fabrics that are sure to delight country-style decorators.

CONSTRUCTION

Divide all the 6½in x 22in pieces of fabric into two groups – one light and one dark. In our sample quilt this was one red/gold group and one blue group.

Working with each group separately, choose two fabrics from the one group and place them right sides together. Mark triangles onto the wrong side of the top fabric exactly as shown in Diagram 1. Note that each triangle must have a base measurement of 3¼in and a height of 2⅞in. Seam allowances are included in these measurements.

These drawn lines, after stitching, will become your cutting lines. Repeat this step using all the fabric pieces.

Stitch the centre seams, using an exact ¼in seam allowance, along the drawn centre line on each pair of fabrics as shown in Diagram 2. Press and cut fabrics on all cutting lines again as shown in Diagram 2.

Press the two triangle units open and save the single triangles for the next step.

ASSEMBLING

Pyramid Units: Remember to keep the light (gold/red) and dark (blue) fabrics separated so that you assemble all light or all dark pyramid units.

Add a single triangle to each side of each two-triangle unit as shown in Diagram 3. This makes a mid-unit.

Join two mid-units as shown in Diagram 4. Then add a further two mid-units to each side as shown in Diagram 5. This forms one pyramid unit.

Continue assembling pyramid units in this manner until you have 24 dark fabric and 30 light fabric pyramids.

Quilt top: Join the nine pyramid units together, alternating light and dark pyramids to form each row. Begin and end each row with a light (red/gold) pyramid. Then join the six rows together to form the quilt top. Refer to the quilt layout diagram.

The dotted lines of triangles on the outside edge of the layout diagram show where these triangles will be trimmed back to a straight edge so the border can be attached. Remember to leave a ¼in seam allowance when trimming these edge triangles back.

ATTACHING THE BORDERS

Cut all the borders down the length of the fabric. All measurements include seam allowances.

For the plain inner border, cut two strips 1½in x 44in and two strips 1½in x 56in.

For the printed fabric border, cut two strips 4½in x 47in and two strips 4½in x 62in.

For the plain outer borders, cut two strips 1½in x 53½in and two strips 1½in x 63in.

Join an inner and outer plain fabric border to each side of a printed fabric border, matching the centre measurements of each border. This will make four separate border units.

Attach one unit to each side of the quilt top. Fold the corners under at a 45-degree angle to mitre corners and stitch.

FINISHED SIZE

- 124cm x 152cm (49in x 60in)

MATERIALS

- 25 light and 25 dark fabric pieces 16.5cm x 56cm (6½in x 22in)
- 1.6m (1¾yd) fabric for printed border
- 1.6m (1¾yd) fabric for plain borders
- 3.2m (3½yd) for backing fabric (this could be the same as printed border and 3.2m would be sufficient for both)
- 132cm x 162cm (52in x 64in) batting to suit
- Sewing threads to blend
- Quilting thread
- Pencil, ruler and basic sewing supplies

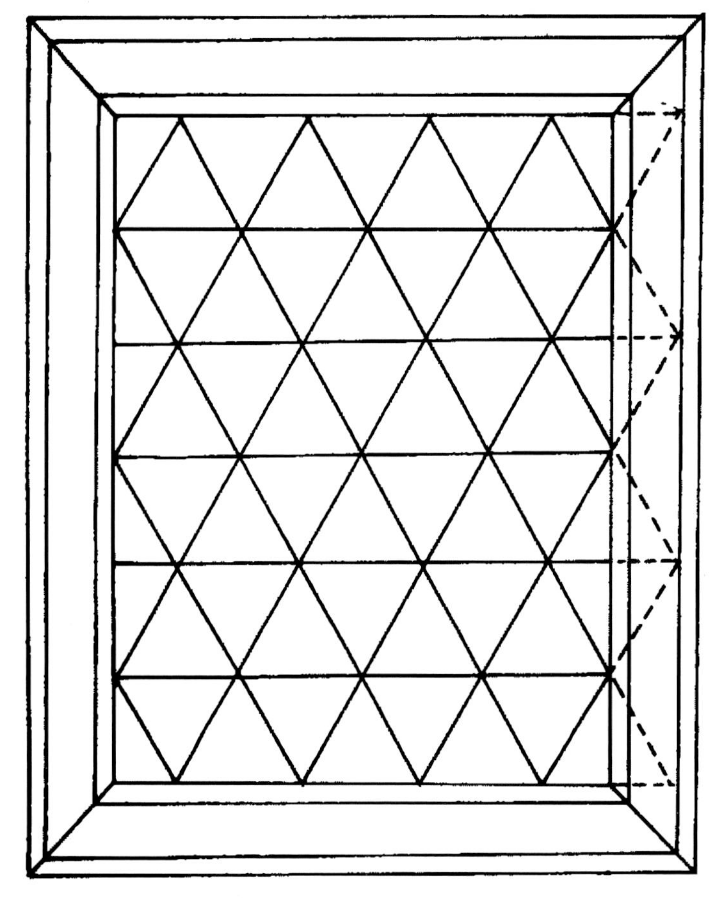

Layout Diagram

BACKING, BINDING AND QUILTING

Cut and join the backing fabric to make a piece 2in bigger all around than the quilt top. These extra inches will allow for any movement that occurs when the layers are tacked together.

Sandwich the backing, wadding and quilt top together and tack the layers ready for quilting. Hand or machine-quilt as desired. Janine has chosen to hand-quilt diamond shapes within each adjoining pair of light or dark pyramids. When quilting is completed, trim the edges of the quilt before attaching the binding.

For the binding, cut 2½in-wide strips from the plain border fabric and join strips to create a finished length of approximately 220in. Iron this length in half lengthwise, wrong sides together. Sew to the front of the quilt, raw edges together. Turn the folded edge to the back and hand-stitch in place.

Sign and date your quilt. ❆

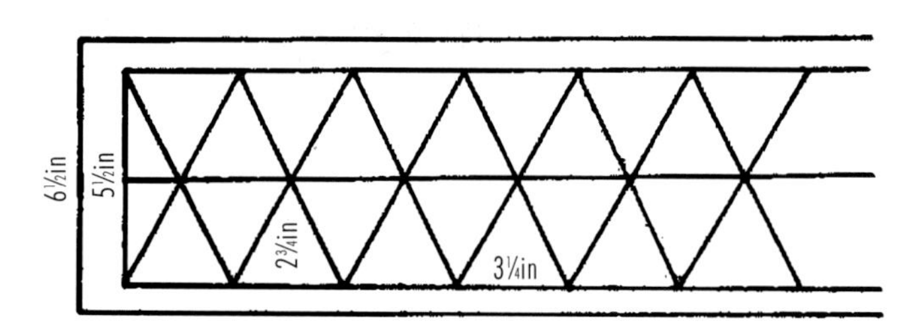

Diagram 1 Mark top fabric only

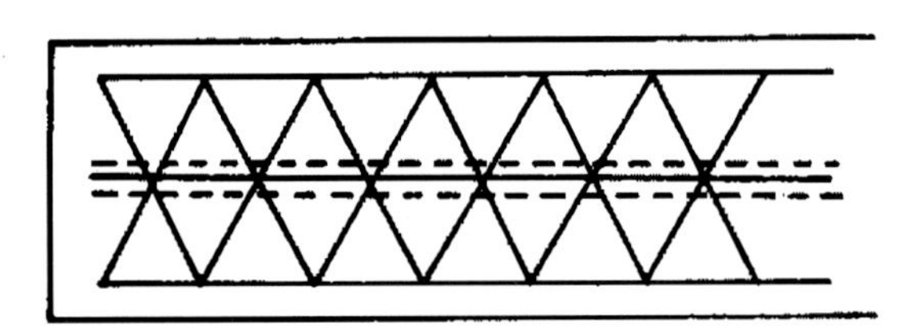

Diagram 2
----- Sewing lines —— Cutting lines

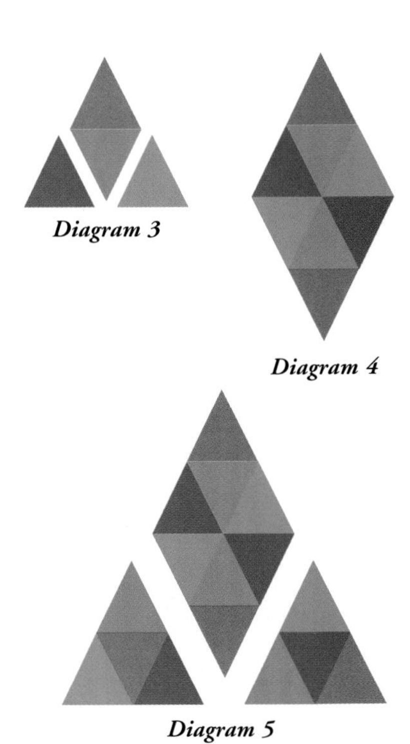

Diagram 3

Diagram 4

Diagram 5

A Bed of Roses

Rose and floral fabrics have a timeless appeal.
Rosemary Walker's beautiful rose quilt is simple to construct
and will lend an air of grace and charm to any home.

PREPARATION

Pre-wash all fabrics and press well. Check that the fabrics have been cut on the cross grain. This quilt is made using the quick strip-piecing method with an accurate ¼in seam.

CUTTING

A ¼in seam allowance has been included in all cutting instructions. When cutting strips, fold each fabric in half, with selvedges together, and cut strips with a grided 24in clear ruler.

Cut the following from the fabrics:

Large floral chintz: Cut nine, 5in strips. Cut each strip into eight, 5in squares to make 72 squares – 70 squares (Block E) will be required for the quilt. Trim the remaining two squares into 3⅞in squares, then cut across these diagonals to make four half-square triangles for the quilt top corners. Next, cut two, 7½in strips and cut each strip into 7½in squares. Finally, recut each square across the diagonals to make 40, quarter-square triangles.

Coloured background print: Cut 12, 2in strips for the nine-patch blocks, six, 3in strips for the inner border and eight, 2½in strips for the binding.

Cream/ivory background print: Cut 12, 2in strips for the nine-patch blocks and seven, 4¾in strips for the outer border.

Cream/ivory homespun: Cut 24, 2in strips for the nine-patch blocks.

CONSTRUCTION

Joining the strips: See the diagrams for the order of joining the strips of the coloured background print, cream/ivory background print and cream/ivory homespun. Press each joined strip carefully, ensuring the seam allowances are pressed to the side of the darker fabric. Try not to distort the long seam.

Cut each of these strips into 2in strips using the 6in square, clear rule which allows for accuracy in 'squaring up' the fabric. These 2in squares will be used for the four colour combinations.

Make up the nine-patch blocks in the four combinations as illustrated. You will require 22 of each different combination. Press well.

ASSEMBLING THE QUILT TOP

The blocks of the quilt are sewn in diagonal lines. Refer to the quilt top construction diagram for placement.

Commence sewing in the top left-hand corner with one Block A joined between two, quarter-square triangles with a half-square triangle sewn to the third side.

ADDING THE BORDERS

Press the quilt well before adding the borders.

Join the strips that were cut from the coloured background print to create one long length for the inner border.

Join the top and bottom inner borders to the quilt top first. Cut sufficient lengths for the top and bottom borders. Pin and sew with the right sides together. Press the seams away towards the darker print.

Repeat for the side borders. Add the outer border in the same way.

FINISHED SIZE

- 65in x 83in (165cm x 211cm)

MATERIALS

- 1.7m (1⅞yd) large-scale floral chintz
- 1.8m (2yd) small/medium print with a coloured background
- 1.6m (1¾yd) small/medium print with cream/ivory background
- 1.3m (1⅜yd) cream/ivory homespun
- Batting – quantity depends on your choice as widths vary. Allow for batting to be approximately 8cm (3in) larger on all sides than the quilt top
- 4.8m (5¼yd) backing fabric
- Machine threads to match dominant colours
- 61cm (24in) clear rule
- 15cm (6in) square, clear rule
- Rotary cutter and mat
- Sewing machine and general sewing supplies
- Walking foot (optional – useful for sewing binding on the quilt)

NOTE: Yardage is estimated for 115cm (45in) wide fabric with allowances made for individual variations in this width and the removal of the selvedges.

NOTE: The small and medium-scale prints should pick up a dominant colour in the large-scale floral print. Rosemary has used unseeded ivory homespun as the fourth fabric. Take care to choose a neutral homespun that blends well with the other fabrics.

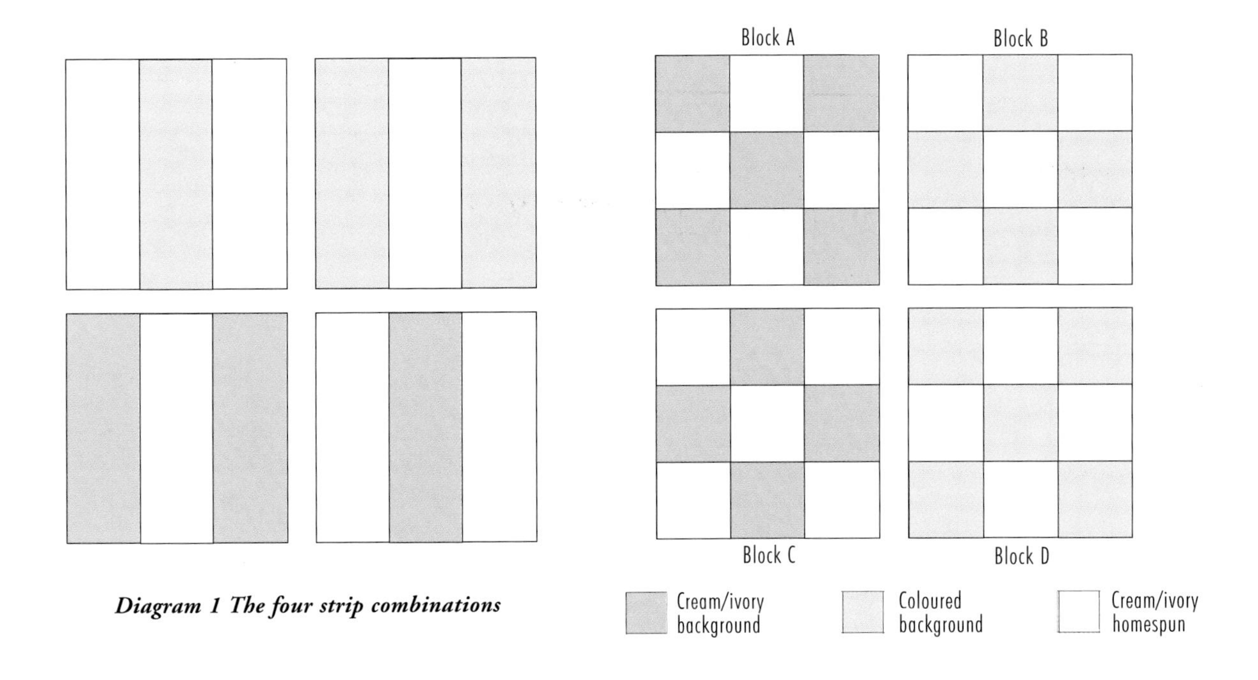

Diagram 1 The four strip combinations

Diagram 2 Quilt Top Construction

There are 18 diagonal rows in the quilt assembly. It is easier to assemble nine rows and put this piece aside. Complete the second set of nine rows and join the two sections together.

QUILTING

This quilt top was quilted using a continuous machine-quilting service. There are many designs from which to choose that will reflect the floral theme of the quilt.

To prepare the quilt for the quilting service, the backing fabric must be cut and joined. Ensure that the backing is 5in larger than the quilt top on all sides.

BINDING

When the quilting is complete, trim away both the excess batting and backing to the edges of the quilt top. Join the binding strips to make one long strip and fold it in half lengthwise.

The binding is sewn first to the top edge, then to the bottom edge. Pin and machine the binding onto the right side of the quilt with a ¼in seam allowance. Then fold the binding to the back of the quilt and slip-stitch in place, catching the machine stitching and the folded edge of the binding.

Repeat for the extra sides of the quilt, leaving an extra 1in of binding at the top and bottom of the quilt. Turn these ends in neatly before slip-stitching the binding in place. This method ensures a well-rounded, filled edge to the binding. ❆

Pansy Cushion

Margaret Cormack has used graded shades of fabrics and traditional appliqué techniques to create the centre design of this colourful cushion. It is the perfect companion for any easy chair.

APPLIQUE TOP

Trace the design outline from the pattern sheet onto the quilter's muslin with a pencil. Remember when tracing the design that the centre square will be 'on point' in the completed cushion. To make the appliqué shapes, trace one whole pansy, one pansy bud and one leaf onto the template plastic with a felt pen. Cut out each individual shape.

Hint: Margaret also traces another copy of the whole pansy and the pansy bud and cuts out just around the outside edge of the entire shape. These extra shapes are a great help when positioning your fabrics.

On the right side of your chosen coloured fabric, draw around the plastic shapes with a sharp pencil. Cut out each shape leaving less than ¼in seam allowance. Spray the pieces lightly with spray starch and press.

Starting with the leaves, finger-press the seam allowance around each piece before placing it on the background fabric. Refer to the diagram on the pattern sheet. You will need to nick the seam allowance on the concave curves as you go. Refer to the numbers on the pattern sheet for piece placement.

Attach some double-sided fusible webbing to the back of the calyx fabric. Draw the calyx shape onto the right side of the fabric and cut it out without a seam allowance.

Iron the calyx to the pansy bud. Blanket-stitch with a single strand of green embroidery cotton around the edge to stop any fraying.

To complete the pansy faces, use two strands of gold thread and Satin-stitch the centres. Work Long Stitches on either

Finger-press the edges of each shape before appliqueing them in place on the traced design. The edges of pieces that will be covered by another piece do not need to be turned under.

FINISHED SIZE

- 45cm (18in) square

BLOCK SIZE

- 30cm (12in)

MATERIALS

- 23cm (9in) square of quilter's muslin
- Small scraps of different green fabric for leaves and pansy calyx
- Scraps of five purple fabrics, ranging from dark to light
- Scraps of five yellow fabrics, ranging from dark to light
- Scraps of five pink fabrics, ranging from dark to light
- 2 x 17.5cm (7in) squares of contrast fabric
- 33cm (13in) square each of Pellon and backing fabric for quilting cushion top
- 30cm (⅓yd) fabric for ruffle
- 34cm x 32cm (13½in x 12½in) rectangle of fabric for cushion back
- Green, gold, cream and black embroidery threads
- Thin template plastic
- Embroidery and kitchen scissors
- Small amount of double-sided fusible webbing to attach calyx on pansy bud
- Appliqué and embroidery needles
- Range of coloured threads to match fabrics
- 35cm (14in) zipper
- No 14 or 16 cushion insert
- Pencil and felt pen
- Spray starch

STITCHES USED

Blanket Stitch, Satin Stitch, Long Stitch

MACHINE-STITCHING THE APPLIQUE

For invisible machine work, use normal thread that matches the background fabric in the bobbin and monofilament thread on top. Smoke-coloured thread should be used for dark fabrics and clear for light.

Set the machine to a blind hem stitch and sew alongside the design, positioning the needle so the stitches are placed just outside the edge of the motif to give a neat appearance.

Alternatively, use a Straight Stitch to appliqué the motif by stitching just inside the outline of the piece. Then cover the stitching line with a zigzag set close enough to create a Satin Stitch finish.

Placing a sheet of unwaxed greaseproof paper behind the background fabric when stitching the appliqué helps to give stability while working and prevents stretching and puckering.

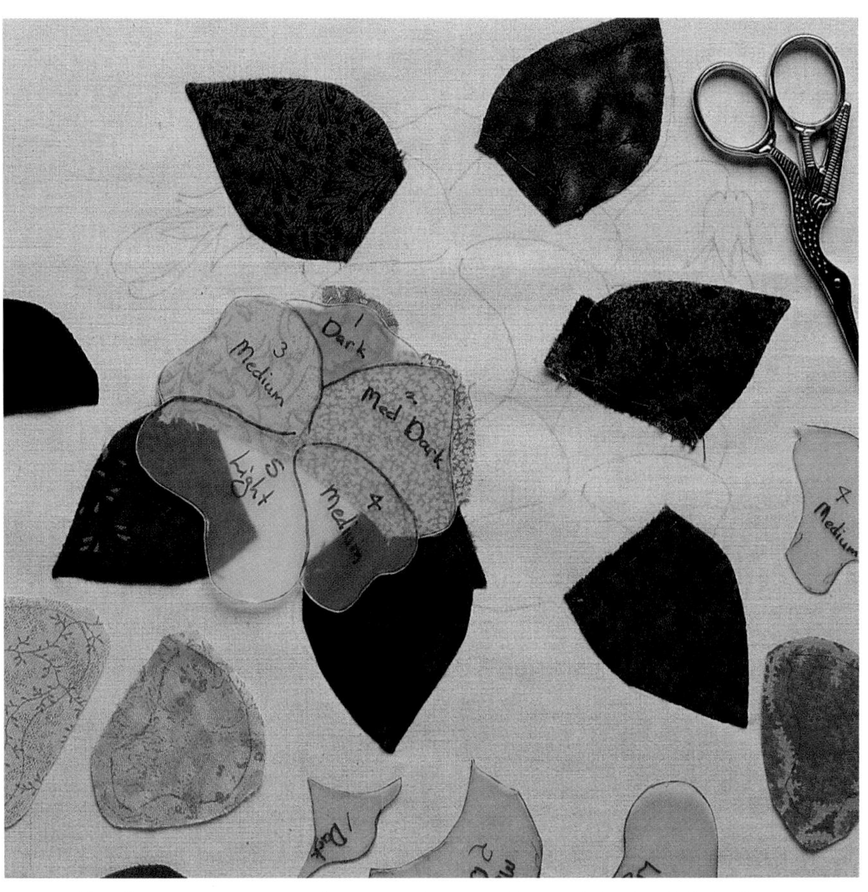

Use the extra pansy template to assist you when positioning fabric shapes ready for appliquéing. You do not need to turn under the seam allowance on sections where pieces of fabric overlap.

side of the gold centres with two strands of cream thread. Using a single strand of black thread, work Long Stitches on the front petal as shown in the colour photograph.

ASSEMBLING THE CUSHION

Cut the two, 7in squares of contrasting fabric in half diagonally to create four triangles. Attach triangles to opposite sides of the appliquéd centre. Press towards the contrast fabric. Repeat the process with the remaining triangles. Sandwich the Pellon square between the appliquéd top and backing fabric. Baste the layers.

Quilt around the outside edge of the appliquéd shapes using small, even running stitches. Trim the Pellon and backing fabric level with the top.

MAKING THE RUFFLE

Cut two, 6in strips across the width of the ruffle fabric. Sew the ends of the strips together to form a circle and press in half lengthwise with the wrong sides and the raw edges together.

Sew two rows of gathering thread along the raw edges. Divide the circle into halves and then quarters, placing a coloured pin or thread at these points. Pull up the gathering threads so the frill fits, distributing gathers evenly. Place the frill onto the front of the cushion, raw edge to raw edge. Sew it to the cushion,

beginning at one side. Pin the ruffle down before attaching the cushion back.

Cut the fabric for the cushion back in half to form two, 12½in x 6¾in rectangles. Press under a ½in seam on one of the long sides of each half.

Using a zipper foot, sew in the zipper, extending it past the ends of the fabric. Place the backing piece, right side up, under the cushion top, then using the stitching line of the ruffle as your guide, sew the two pieces together. Start on one side of the zipper, then as you get close to the other side, undo the zipper three or four inches, before sewing over the last part. Turn the cushion right side out and put in the cushion insert. ❆

William's Quilt

Using serviceable navy as a base and a scrap bag of colourful checks and plaids, Margaret Cormack has used half-square triangles to create this versatile quilt.

Note: A ¼in seam allowance is used throughout this quilt. William's quilt features 20 blocks arranged four across and five down. Each block is made up of 16 half-square triangles.

CUTTING

Using the navy fabric, cut 20, 3⅞in strips across the width of the fabric. Crosscut each of these strips into 10, 3⅞in squares. Then cut the squares across the diagonal to give a total of 400 navy triangles. Also from the navy fabric, cut six, 1½in strips across the width of the fabric for the first border.

From the scraps of check fabrics, cut 200, 3⅞in squares. Cut the squares across the diagonal to give a total of 400 check triangles.

PIECING THE BLOCKS

With right sides together, join the navy and check triangles together as shown in Diagram 1. Chain-piecing the pairs through your machine will save time and cotton. Cut the chain-pieced pairs apart and press open with the seam allowance towards the navy fabric. Be careful not to stretch the seam when pressing.

Divide the half-square triangles into colour groups. Each block will require 16 squares of similar-colour checks.

Lay out each block and then join the squares into four rows of four blocks each. Refer to the block-piecing and block diagrams.

ASSEMBLING THE QUILT

Lay out your completed blocks with four across and five down. The blocks of a similar colour are placed diagonally through the quilt.

Join rows of blocks together, then join the rows. Use the photograph as a guide.

MAKING THE BORDER

For the border you will need 72 half-square triangles. For each of the side borders join 20 squares together as shown in Diagram 2.

Join two, 1½in strips of navy together for each side. You will need about a 60½in strip. Stitch the strip to the check side of your border, then press the seams towards the navy fabric.

Pin and stitch the strips to the sides of the quilt and press the seam towards the navy border.

For each of the top and bottom borders, join 16 half-square triangles.

To make the four corner blocks, attach a 1½in x 3½in strip of navy fabric to one half-square triangle as shown in Diagram 3. You will need two of each type. Attach these blocks to the end of the top and bottom border strips.

Join the excess navy strip, cut off from the side borders, to a full strip, then attach the navy strip to the check side of the top and bottom borders.

Attach these borders to the top and bottom of your quilt. Press the seam towards the navy strip. Refer to Diagram 4.

FINISHED SIZE

- 144cm x 174cm (56½in x 68½in)

BLOCK SIZE

- 30cm (12in)

MATERIALS

- 3m (3¼yd) navy cotton fabric
- Scraps of check fabric in a variety of colours (you need 16 similar colour checks for each of the blocks)
- 152cm x 182cm (60in x 72in) of batting
- 3m (3¼yd) backing fabric
- Rotary cutter, ruler and mat
- Navy quilting thread

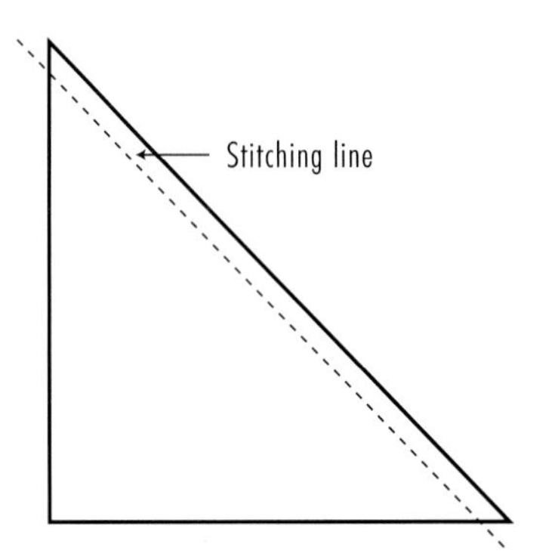

***Diagram 1** Join the navy and check triangles together along the diagonal.*

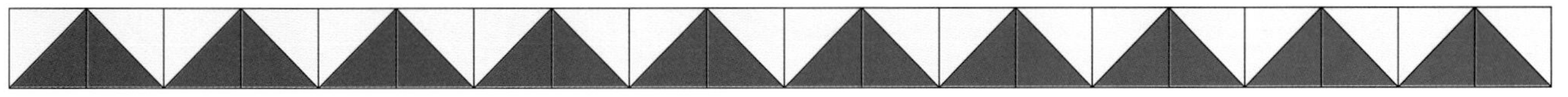

***Diagram 2** For each of the borders, join 20 half-square triangles together.*

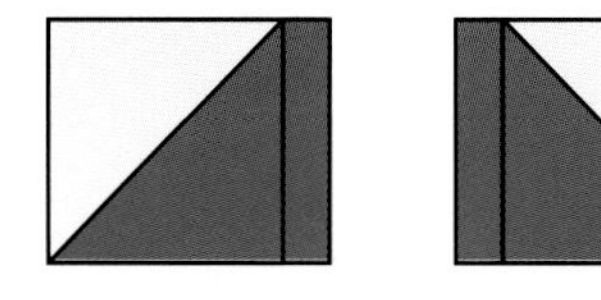

Diagram 3 Attach a 1½in x 3½in strip to half-square triangles.

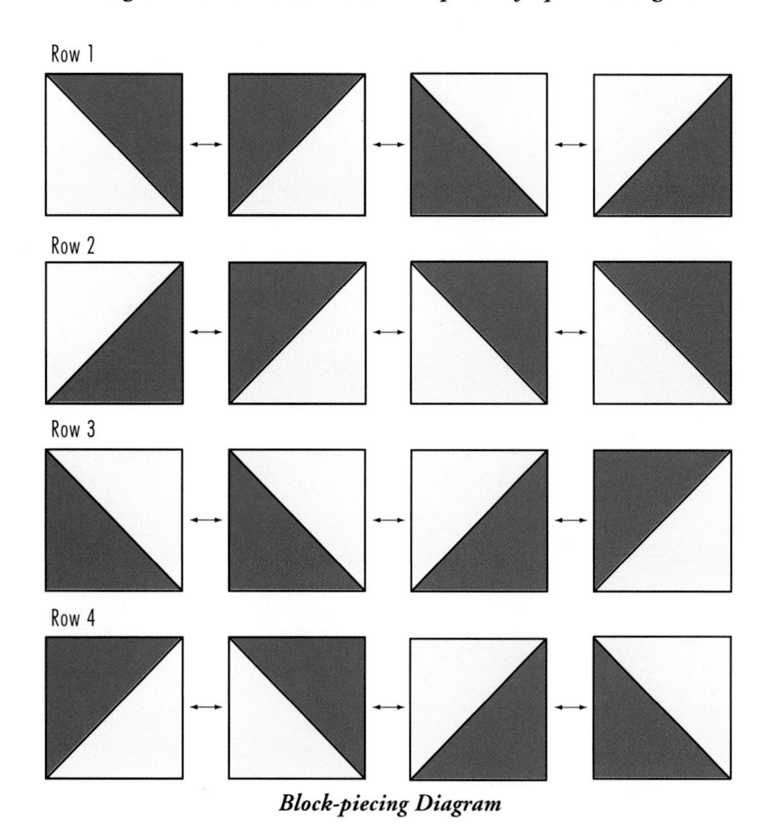

Block-piecing Diagram

Block Diagram

Quilt Block

Diagram 4 Attach the corner blocks to the end of the top and bottom border strips.

Piecing the Blocks

QUILTING AND BINDING

Layer your backing, batting and quilt top together. Baste the three layers together and then quilt as desired. Margaret has quilted ¼in inside each triangle with navy quilting thread.

When your quilting is complete, trim away the excess wadding and backing fabric to 1in from the quilt edge.

Cut six, 5in strips of navy fabric. Join two strips to form one long strip. Repeat with another two strips. Press both strips in half lengthwise.

Measure the length of the quilt through the centre. Cut two strips to this length, then pin and sew to the sides of the quilt through all three layers. Press away from the quilt top.

Join the off-cut strips to the other two full-length strips. Press these in half lengthwise. Measure the width of your quilt, adding 4½in to the total measurement. Cut two strips to this length and join these strips to the top and bottom of the quilt. Press. Starting with the sides, turn the folded edge to the back of the quilt and hand-stitch in place. ❆

A Stitcher's Collection

Christine Book designed this small wall quilt to display a collection of hand-stitched treasures such as embroidered doilies, crocheted pieces and antique glass buttons. She used colours and images associated with the 1930s, continuing the theme with bright pastel reproduction fabrics, a 1930s-style quilt block and glass buttons.

Note: A ¼in seam allowance is used throughout. All fabrics are 100 per cent cotton and are pre-washed and ironed.

PIECING AND STITCHING THE BACKGROUND

The background of this small wall quilt was made simply using only three fabrics. When choosing fabric for the quilt background, select uncomplicated prints so as not to distract from the treasures on display.

Following the layout diagram on the pattern sheet, cut out the three sections for the quilt top. Pin and stitch Sections A and B together and then stitch these to Section C to form the quilt top.

Lay the backing fabric wrong side up on a table, place the batting on the backing fabric and then place the quilt top, right side up, on top. Ensure all the layers are lying flat and smooth, then pin or tack them together to prevent movement while quilting.

The quilt has been hand-quilted in a diagonal grid pattern with lines 2in apart. Lightly pencil on the quilting lines. If you do not wish to mark the quilt top, the straight quilting lines can be marked with lengths of masking tape. After you have quilted along the edge of a length of masking tape you can gently pull it away. If you prefer, you can machine-quilt using a walking foot on your sewing machine or take your quilt to a professional continuous machine-quilter for stipple/meander quilting.

BINDING

Once your quilt has been completed, trim the excess backing fabric and batting level with your quilt top. It is recommended that you check your measurements again to ensure the quilt is square.

To give this quilt a scrap-patchwork effect, the binding has been randomly pieced from 1930s reproduction fabric. To do this, cut a variety of 2½in-wide strips of differing lengths on the straight grain, then join them together to form the length required for each side of your quilt. Chris has used 12 different fabrics. Fold these binding strips in half lengthwise, wrong sides together, and press. Place the raw edges of the binding strip along the raw edges of the top of the quilt, right side up and pin in place. Using a 1½in seam, stitch the binding to the front of the quilt top. Turn the binding to the back and hand-stitch in place. Repeat for the bottom of the quilt. Attach the side bindings in the same manner, leaving 12in of binding overhanging at either end. Turn these ends in neatly before slip-stitching the binding in place.

Your quilt is now complete and ready to have all your treasures stitched in place. This quilt is intended to inspire you, so only instructions for its key elements are included.

Adapt these ideas, rearrange the placement of the sewing trinkets and experiment until you reach an overall design that pleases you and complements your individual collection.

EMBELLISHMENTS

Appliqued Pinwheel Block: This patchwork block is a feature because it is a traditional 1930s block and also 'shows off' a variety of colourful fabrics. Using the template outlines on the pattern sheet, make lightweight cardboard templates for the circle and each of the wedge shapes. Cut out eight different

FINISHED SIZE

- 58.5cm x 71cm (23in x 28in)

MATERIALS

- Three pieces of light/neutral fabrics for quilt background:
  Section A – 21.5cm x 51cm (8½in x 20in)
  Section B – 38cm x 51cm (15in x 20in)
  Section C – 58cm x 24cm (23in x 9½in)
- Assorted fabric scraps for appliqué
- Assorted lengths of old-fashioned lace
- Two or more old-fashioned fancy doilies
- Assortment of sewing treasures to include (see suggestions list)
- 2.75m (3yd) of assorted scraps of 1930s reproduction fabric for quilt binding
- 70cm x 80cm (27⅝in x 31½in) lightweight fabric for backing
- 70cm x 80cm (27⅝in x 31½in) piece of thin batting
- Polyester filling
- Quilting cotton
- Assorted embroidery threads
- Lightweight cardboard for templates
- Permanent marker for tracing designs
- Pencil
- Masking tape
- Rotary cutter, ruler and board
- General sewing supplies

STITCHES USED

Backstitch, Hemstitch

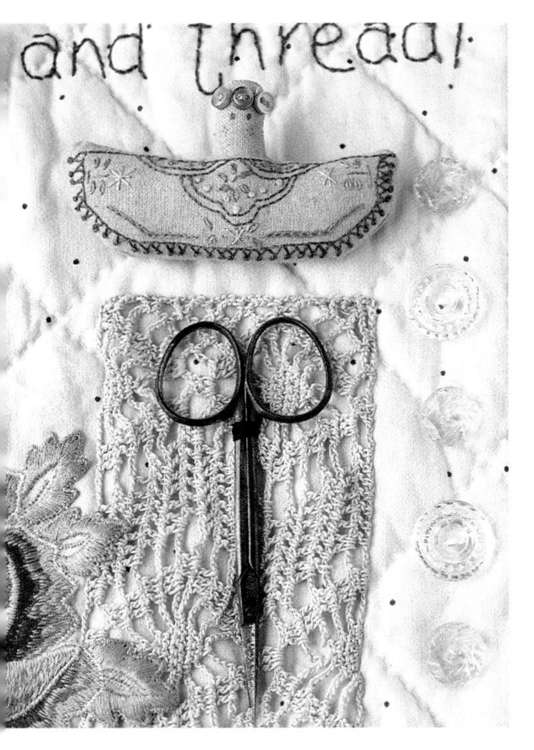

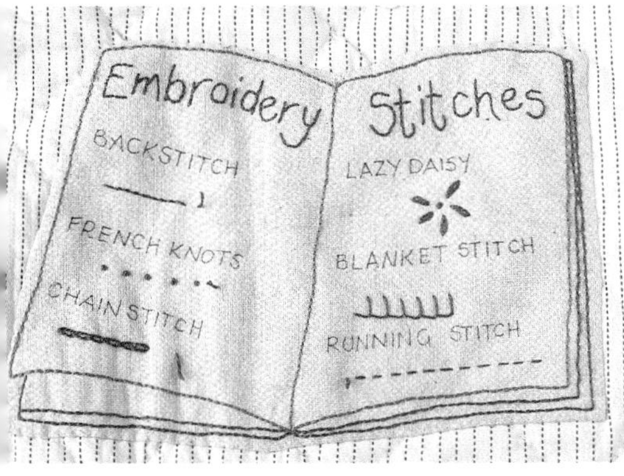

fabrics for the wedges of the pinwheel and one piece of fabric for the centre circle, allowing a ¼in seam allowance for each piece. Turn the seam allowance under and baste. Press each piece. Join the wedges by top-stitching together using a neutral thread. Once all wedge shapes are sewn together, appliqué the centre circle into position. Remove the tacking and carefully pull out the cardboard templates. Pin the pinwheel into position, then appliqué in place using a small, invisible Blind Hemstitch. Ensure that your stitching is on the quilt top and does not show from the back.

Appliquéd Button Jar: This design is the perfect place to show off a special button collection.

Trace the 'Buttons' lettering from the pattern sheet onto the light fabric. Using six strands of an embroidery thread of your choice, work the letters in a small, even Backstitch. Trace the jar shape and lid from the pattern sheet onto lightweight cardboard and cut out.

Cover these templates with your chosen fabric, ensuring the lettering is centred on the jar. and press. Appliqué the jar shape into position, with the template in or out depending on your preferred appliqué method. Once you have sewn the jar into position, appliqué the jar lid onto the quilt. Backstitch the jar details using two strands of black embroidery thread. Position your buttons and stitch onto the bottom of the jar.

Doily Flap Pocket: This is the blue pocket on the lower right-hand side of the quilt and is useful for storing treasures and little sewing secrets. This small pocket features the embroidered end of a doily as the flap. To make this pocket, cut a rectangle from your chosen fabric that measures 10in x 7¼in. Machine-stitch a ¼in hem, turned twice, along one of the 10in sides – this will become the top opening of the pocket. Fold the rectangle in half, right sides together, so that the 7¼in sides meet. Machine-stitch a ¼in seam down the raw edge of the 7¼in side and along the bottom edge. Turn the pocket right side out.

Decide how much of your doily you will need to make the pocket's flap and cut your doily where required, remembering to leave enough fabric to attach the flap. Hand-stitch the flap into position on the back of the pocket bag so the embroidered section forms a flap at the front of the pocket.

Next, carefully hand-appliqué your pocket into position on the quilt, stitching around all four sides. (Chris has stitched a small crocheted drawstring bag with a thimble inside to a corner of the pocket which contains a selection of antique threads.)

Heart Pincushion: The heart pincushion hangs from an old buckle on the top right-hand corner of the quilt. To achieve an authentically old and worn look, cut 1½in squares from a variety of fabrics. Piece these squares into a rectangle measuring 4in x 6in. Tea-stain the patchwork piece. The patchwork has been hand-quilted, using thin wadding, in a diagonal grid pattern with lines ⅝in apart.

Select another piece of fabric for the pincushion backing and, on the wrong side, trace the heart pattern from the pattern sheet. With the patchwork fabric and backing fabric right sides together, stitch around the heart on the traced line, leaving a small opening for turning on one side.

Trim, clip and turn right side out. Stuff the heart firmly with polyester filling and stitch the opening closed. Trim with some old rickrack braid around the heart so that it can hang from the buckle. A length of tape-measure ribbon and some wooden spools could also hang from the buckle.

Embroidery Book: This is worked on old linen, however you can get the same aged look by tea-staining a small piece of calico. Using the book template from the pattern sheet, trace the design onto your fabric. A fine-point permanent marker is ideal to draw the design. Backstitch all the book pages and the words 'Embroidery Stitches'. The names of the stitches are simply written with a fine-point permanent marker. Work a few examples of the stitches in the space below each name. Tuck a small hem around your stitching and appliqué your embroidery book into position.

Embroidered Phrase: Using the design for the phrase included on the pattern sheet as a guide, write directly onto your quilt with a pencil, wherever you have a space. Using two strands of embroidery thread, embroider the phrase in a small, even Backstitch. You could also embroider a bow and hanging hearts design in other spaces you have available.

ADDING OTHER BITS AND PIECES

Other ideas for embellishments include:

- Adding appliquéd crochet pieces and decorative buttons
- Embroidering your name, date and the quilt's title onto a fancywork doily then appliquéing this onto the quilt
- Rows of decorative lace can be stitched in place along the quilt's edge and mother-of-pearl buttons added
- Make some yoyos (a gathered circle) from old, interesting fabric and stitch on
- The needle case has been made from a crocheted crinoline lady which was purchased at a fete
- An old, pink crocheted compact case has been used as a pocket for your embroidery scissors
- Pin some old brooches onto your quilt

Finally, remember that this is an inspirational quilt and have fun hunting for all the treasures your quilt will contain. This is the type of project that may never be finished – you can keep adding treasures that come your way! ❃

SUGGESTIONS FOR YOUR COLLECTION QUILT:

- Embroidered, crocheted or fancywork doilies
- Buttons – glass and mother-of-pearl in a variety of interesting shapes
- Old ribbons such as grosgrain or new novelty ribbons
- Quilt blocks and appliqués
- Embroidered motifs
- Embroidered pieces to cut up for pocket fronts and flaps
- Interesting pieces of jewellery
- Packets of needles, small embroidery scissors, wooden spools and skeins of embroidery floss
- Rickrack and old-fashioned braids

Summer Trellis

Lazy summer afternoons in the garden are evoked by the soft colours of the flowers, the rich green of the trellis and the cool white of the background in this quilt designed and stitched by Tricia Sewell.

FINISHED SIZE

- 99cm (39in) square

BLOCK SIZE

- 25.4cm (10in)

MATERIALS

- Template plastic (thick and thin)
- 2B pencil
- 1m (1⅛yd) white background fabric
- 1m (1⅛yd) border stripe fabric
- 2m (2¼yd) small floral fabric
- 1m (1⅛yd) medium floral fabric (or sufficient to get eight rectangles for Template A)
- Scraps of cotton fabric for centre appliqué

Note: This quilt is made using imperial measurements. A (6mm) ¼in seam allowance is used throughout. The templates do not allow for this seam allowance, you must add it when cutting.

PIECING THE BLOCKS

Trace Templates A to E onto thick plastic and accurately cut out the shapes, allowing a ¼in seam allowance. Use a sharp pencil to transfer the shapes onto the appropriate fabrics.

Note: Template A is a rectangle, not a square, and must be sewn with its longer side horizontal as shown in the piecing diagram.

For each block, cut and sew the following. Cut one A from the medium floral fabric. Cut two Bs and two Cs from the white background fabric and add the Bs to the top and bottom of A. Add Cs to the remaining shorter sides of A. Cut four Ds from the narrow bands of the border stripe fabric. Sew these to the block so that the long side of D fits to the side of the white C and Bs. Complete the block by cutting four E pieces from the white background fabric and sewing to the D pieces. Follow the piecing diagram. Make eight blocks in all.

THE CENTRE BLOCK

Cut the white background material for the centre block at least 1in bigger all around than required (at least 12in square). Lightly trace the pattern outline onto the front of the background fabric, being careful to centre the appliqué design. Using scraps of fabric, begin with the flower stems and appliqué with matching cotton using a fine Blind Stitch.

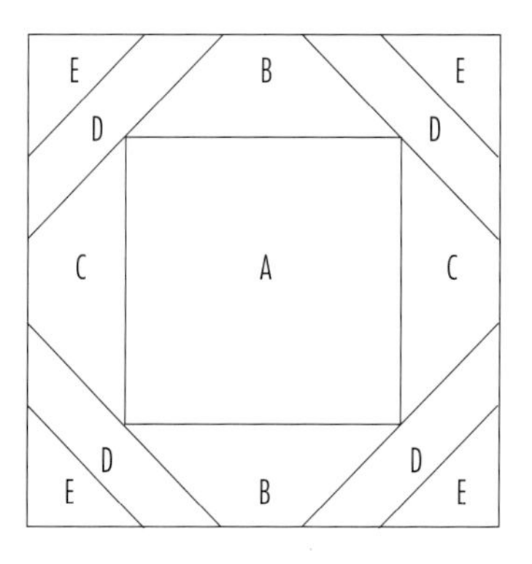

Follow this diagram to complete the trellis blocks.

Join Templates A to E to make eight pieced trellis blocks.

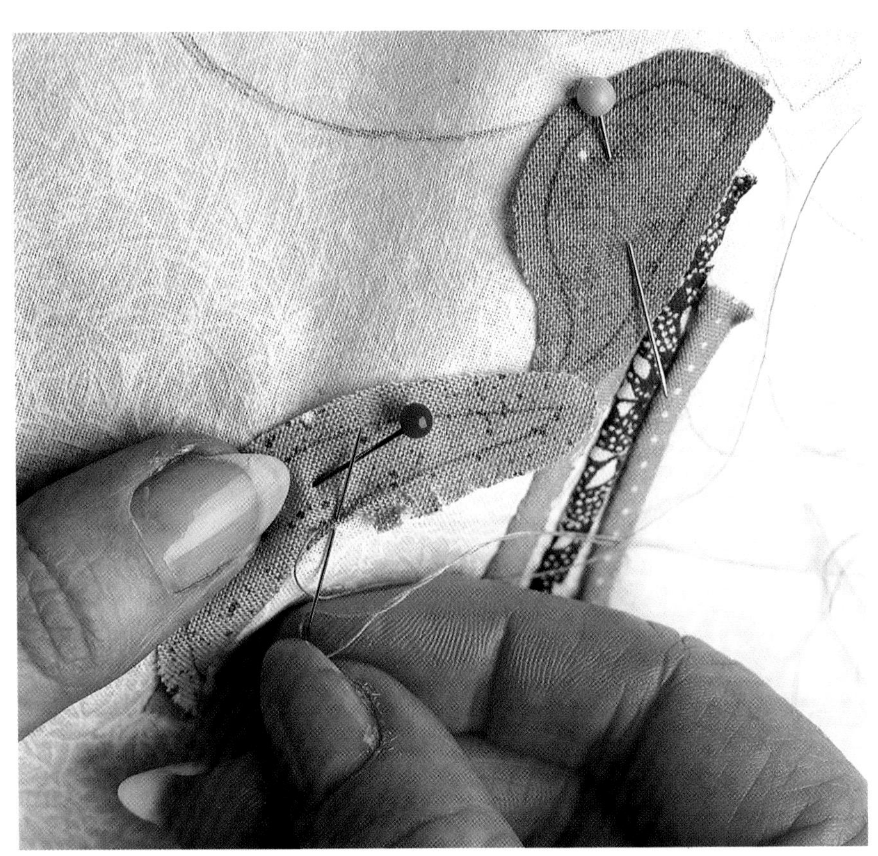

Pin appliqué pieces in place and needle-turn seam allowances.

Finish appliquéing the bow, then the flowers, taking note of the pieces that will be covered by others.

When the appliqué is finished, use Template F to mark sewing lines on the back of the completed appliqué. From the small print fabric, cut four triangles (Template E) and sew them to the corners of the appliquéd block to complete the square.

ASSEMBLING THE SQUARE

Before starting to assemble the blocks, check that all blocks have Template A lying the same way. For Row 1, sew three pieced blocks together in a strip (refer to photograph), being careful to match all the seams.

For Row 2, sew one pieced block to one side of the appliquéd block to the other side so that the appliqué is in the middle. Again, match all seams. Row 3 is the same as Row 1.

Join the first and second rows and sew across in one long seam, pinning all seams carefully before sewing. To complete, add the third row, ensuring that the appliqué remains in the centre. Check to see that the quilt measures 30in square.

ADDING BORDERS

From the small print fabric, cut two borders 1in x 30in plus seam allowances and two borders 1in x 32in plus seam allowances. From the border stripe fabric, cut four (wide band) borders measuring 3½in x 39in plus seam allowances. Pin in place and sew on, mitring the corners as you go.

FINISHING

Iron the whole quilt carefully. Lightly trace on your preferred quilting pattern. The sample quilt has been quilted ¼in from the edge of the blocks and again 1in further in.

The centre block white background has been quilted in a cross hatch design, with the small floral corners quilted ¼in from the edges. A diagram for the bow pattern on the corners is given on the pattern sheet. Use the small floral fabric for the backing and binding.

Cut the backing and batting one to two inches larger all around than the finished top. Baste the three layers together and quilt as desired.

Square the finished quilt and add the binding, cutting it 2½in wide and approximately 160in long. Iron the binding in half, and after pinning it in place, machine-sew to the edge of the quilt, mitring each corner. Slip-stitch the binding on the back of the quilt. ❆

All quilts courtesy of Narelle Grieve and Margaret Cormack.

Country Classics

Chooks in Clover

This country-style table throw or wall-hanging captures the essence of rural life with its friendly chooks and colourful flowers. Incorporating easy patchwork and naive appliqué techniques, our decorative throw was designed by The Chook Shed Pattern Co.

PIECING THE CENTRE BLOCK

From your assorted medium and dark fabric scraps, cut 48, 2½in squares. Sort the squares into sets of four and join each set to form a four-patch unit. Make four units. From your light fabric scraps, cut five, 4½in squares. Join the four-patch units and light squares in an alternate sequence as shown in Diagram 1.

ATTACHING THE INNER BORDER

Again, from the medium and dark fabric scraps, cut 28, 2½in squares. Join 12 squares together into two strips of six squares each and join to either side of the centre block. From the remaining 16 squares, make two strips of eight blocks and attach to the top and bottom of the centre block.

ADDING THE APPLIQUE BORDER

From the background fabric, cut two, 10½in x 36½in strips and attach to the top and bottom of the quilt. It is a good idea to check these measurements against your quilt before cutting. This will allow for any minor discrepancies in individual cutting and piecing techniques.

OUTER BORDER

Cut 76, 2½in squares from your medium and dark fabric scraps. Join 18 squares for each side border, attach to the quilt and press. Then, join 20 squares for the top and bottom borders and attach to the quilt.

APPLIQUE SHAPES

Trace the appliqué shapes shown on the pattern sheet onto the paper side of the double-sided fusible webbing. Cut the shapes out, approximately ¼in outside the traced line. Iron the shapes onto the wrong side of your chosen fabrics and then cut out the shapes on the traced lines. Peel off the backing paper and arrange the shapes on the background fabrics. Refer to the colour photograph. When you are completely happy with your placement and colours, press the shapes into place with a warm iron.

Buttonhole-stitch around each shape using two strands of embroidery thread. Alternatively, if you have a sewing machine with a decorative stitch, machine-stitch around each shape.

QUILTING

Cut your backing fabric to a size 2in larger all around than the quilt top. Tape the backing fabric face down onto a table

FINISHED SIZE

- 102cm (40in) square

BLOCK SIZE

- 25.4cm (10in)

MATERIALS

- 1m (1⅛yd) background fabric for the appliqué border
- Assorted medium and dark fabric scraps for the 120 scrappy squares
- Assorted light fabric scraps for the five centre appliqué squares
- Assorted fabrics for appliqué shapes
- 30cm (⅓yd) fabric for binding
- 1.15m (1¼yd) backing fabric
- 115cm (45in) square of batting
- Stranded embroidery thread in various colours to complement fabrics
- 60cm (⅝yd) double-sided fusible webbing
- General sewing supplies

STITCHES USED

Buttonhole Stitch, Backstitch

or the floor, then smooth out all the creases. Lay the batting over the backing fabric, then place the quilt top right side up. Smooth out and pin the fabrics together with safety pins or tack through all three layers to hold them in place while quilting.

Quilt as desired. Our quilt has been quilted in the ditch of the seamlines around the pieced areas and appliqué shapes, and stipple machine-quilted between the chooks and flowers.

BINDING

When your quilting is complete, trim the backing and wadding level with the quilt top. Cut four, 2½in strips across the width of the fabric. Join the lengths using a bias seam. Fold the strips in half lengthwise, wrong sides together and press. Place the raw edges of the binding strip along the raw edge of the quilt, starting halfway along one side. Using a ¼in seam, stitch

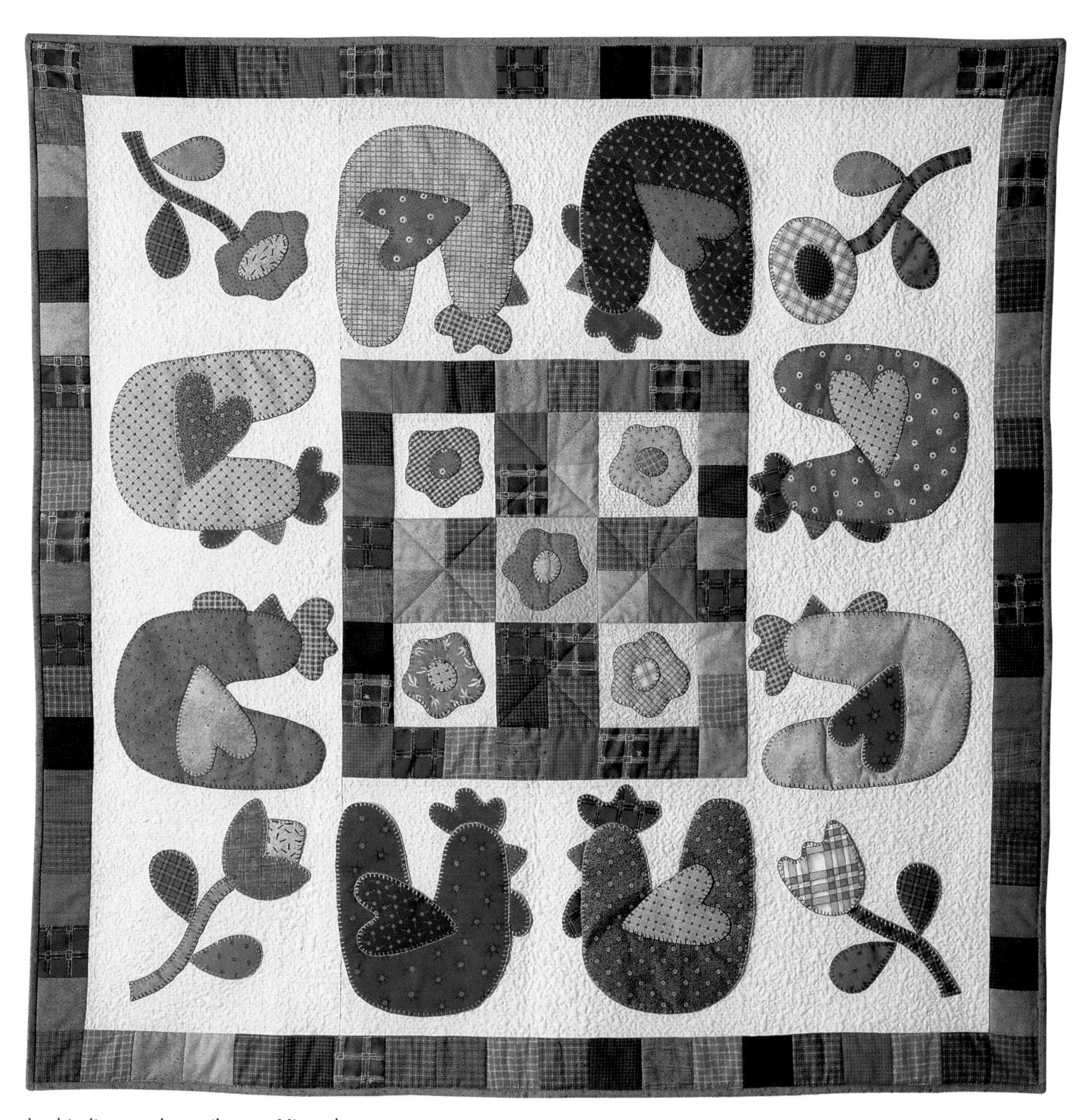

the binding to the quilt top. Mitre the corners by stopping ¼in from the corner, sew a Backstitch, then remove the quilt from the machine.

Fold the binding straight up (away from the quilt), then straight down and start stitching again along the edge of the quilt. Repeat this for the other three corners. Join the end of the binding to make a neat finish. Turn the binding to the back of the quilt and hand-stitch in place. Date and label your new quilt. ❆

Diagram 1

Log Cabin Quilt

Virginia Edwards has used foundation piecing to create her charming Barn Raising Log Cabin Quilt, adorned with sweet heirloom buttons.

Note: The Log Cabin design needs a selection of light and dark fabrics. In this quilt, the light fabrics ranged from creams through to pinks and apricots. The dark fabrics were many shades of green with touches of red and black for depth.

There are more than 100 different coloured fabrics, some only small scraps, in this quilt.

PREPARATION

Trace the Log Cabin foundation diagram onto paper using a thin black permanent marker. Wash and iron the lightweight cotton foundation fabric. From the foundation fabric, cut 64, 23cm (9in) squares. Lay each square over the traced paper pattern and trace the diagram onto the fabric.

CONSTRUCTION

Make sure you refer to the diagram and place light and dark strips accordingly and then sew these in order from 1-16.

Take one centre square and lay right side up on the back of the foundation fabric, lining up the square within the drawn lines.

Place the first light strip 1 over the centre square and pin in place. Flip the square of foundation fabric over and sew along the drawn line, creating the first seam. Turn your block over and iron the first strip down flat, trimming any excess fabric from the strip. Lay the light strip 2 face down over strip 1 and repeat the process until all 16 strips are sewn down. Use the diagram and the photograph as a guide to block construction. When the block is done, trim the four outer strips back to 4cm (1½in). Continue in this way until 64 blocks are completed.

FINISHED SIZE

- 193cm (76in) square

BLOCK SIZE

- 187mm (8in) square

MATERIALS

- Large assortment of light and dark fabrics – prints and plains, cut into 4cm (1½in) wide strips
- 64, 5cm (2in) squares of dark fabric
- 4m (4½yd) of lightweight cotton lawn or voile in cream or white for foundation fabric
- 1.6m (1¾yd) green spotted fabric for first border
- 1.7m (1⅞yd) cream and floral fabric for second border
- 2m (2¼yd) black floral fabric for third border
- 2m (2¼yd) square of batting
- 4m x 115cm (4⅜yd x 45in) backing fabric
- Marking pen
- Rotary cutter, mat and ruler
- Beige or grey thread
- Embroidery cotton
- Sewing machine and basic sewing supplies
- Collection of old or interesting buttons

STITCHES USED

Buttonhole Stitch

NOTE: Use either metric or imperial measurements throughout.

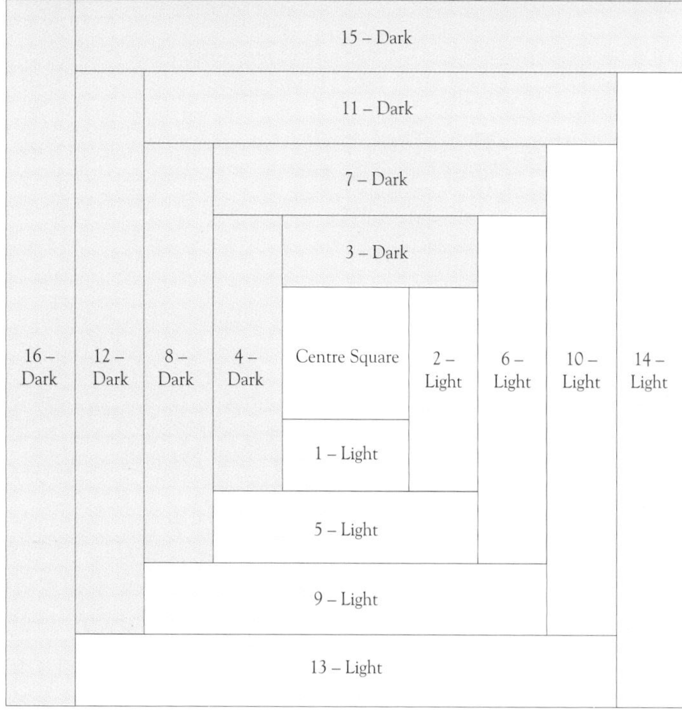

Foundation Diagram

ASSEMBLY

Arrange the 64 blocks according to the design photograph. These blocks are sewn together in eight rows of eight blocks.

When sewing the rows, iron the seams in alternate directions. When you come to sew the rows together, the seam allowances will then butt up against each other, matching the seams. Continue until all eight rows are sewn together.

ADDING THE BORDERS

Border 1: Measure the edges of the first assembled quilt top and then cut the first borders into 6.5cm x 153.5cm (2½in x 60in) strips and attach.

Border 2: From a light fabric, cut 9cm (3½in) strips as long as the measured areas, approximately 163cm (64in), and attach to border 1.

Border 3: Again, measure the side edges of the quilt and cut four, 11.5cm x 193cm (4½in x 76in) strips from the dark fabric. Sew these onto the sides of quilt.

ASSEMBLING THE QUILT

Cut the backing fabric in half, removing all the selvedges, and sew the pieces together along the longer side. Iron the seams open. Sandwich the backing, batting and quilt, then pin with safety pins.

TYING AND BUTTONING

As a foundation-pieced quilt has more layers than a traditionally-pieced quilt, it

is rather difficult to hand-quilt through all the layers. Virginia's chosen option was to tie and button this quilt.

Place the pinned quilt in a frame and, with a large-eyed needle and matching embroidery or Perlé thread, tie each block in the middle of the outer four strips. Attach an interesting button to the middle of the centre square. You may choose to quilt the borders with an appropriate pattern to enhance the quilt.

BINDING

From border fabric 1, cut 6.5cm (2½in) strips. Join these until you have enough binding to go around the quilt plus some extra – about 8m (8¾yd).

Press in half, wrong sides together and sew the binding to the right sides of the quilt, mitring the corners, and Slip-stitch into place. ❆

Springtime Baskets

This charming quilt uses both piecing and appliqué techniques to create a delightful effect. Designed by Country Pieces, it's a wall-hanging with lasting appeal.

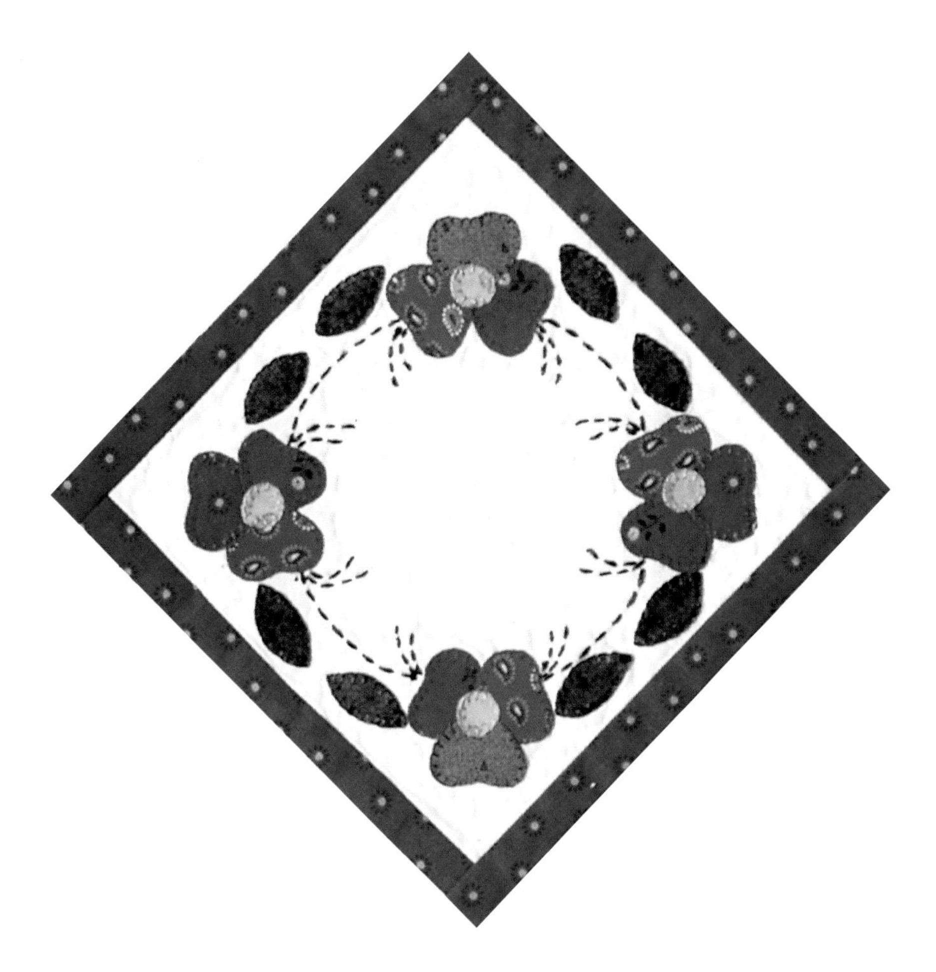

FINISHED SIZE

- 58.5cm (23in) square

BLOCK SIZE

- 25.4cm (10in)

MATERIALS

- 46cm x 107cm (18in x 42in) cream background fabric
- 20cm x 107cm (8in x 42in) blue fabric for sashings and first border – cut 20cm (8in) off one end to use in the piecing and appliqué
- 20cm x 107cm (8in x 42in) red fabric for second border – cut 20cm (8in) off one end to use in pattern 5, 6 and appliqué
- Assorted 20cm (8in) squares in mauve, light print, light brown, mid green, deep green (basket base and leaves), mustard and mid-red
- Double-sided fusible webbing
- Embroidery threads to match the reds, mauve, blue and dark green
- 63.5cm (25in) square of thin batting
- 63.5cm (25in) square of backing fabric
- Cutting board, ruler and rotary cutter
- Thin cardboard or template plastic
- Scissors

STITCHES USED

Buttonhole Stitch, Running Stitch

NOTE: Please read the instructions carefully before commencing and use a ¼in seam allowance throughout this project. There are two colourways in the baskets and flowers.
A ¼in seam allowance has been added to all pattern pieces.

CUTTING INSTRUCTIONS

Transfer the templates for pattern pieces 1, 2, 3, 4, 5, 7 and 8 from the pattern sheet onto thin cardboard or template plastic. See below for cutting pattern 6, 9 and 10.

From the plain cream homespun fabric:

- 4 x pattern 7 and 4 x pattern 8 (left and right sides of basket blocks)
- 2, 7in squares – then cut each square on the diagonal into two triangles basket handle (pattern 10)
- 2, 2⅞in squares – then cut each square on the diagonal into two triangles basket base section (pattern 9)
- 1, 6½in square – centre appliqué block
- 2, 6in squares – corner triangles
- 2, 8in squares – filler triangles

Then cut the 6in and the 8in squares along the diagonal into two triangles.

From the deep-red fabric:

- 2, 2⅞in squares, cut into two triangles (pattern 6) as for deep red

From the blue fabric:

- 2 x pattern 1
- 4 petals

From the light floral fabric:

- 2 x pattern 2
- 2 x pattern 3

From the mid-green fabric:

- 2 x pattern 3

From the light brown fabric:

- 2 x pattern 4

From the mid-red fabric:

- 2 x pattern 2
- 8 petals

From the purple fabric:

- 2 x pattern 4

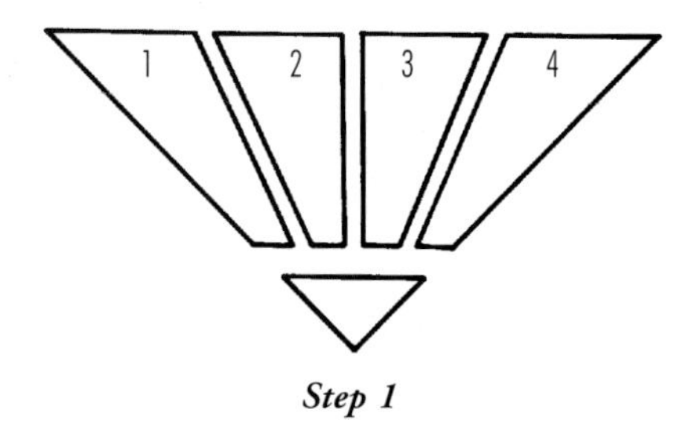

Step 1

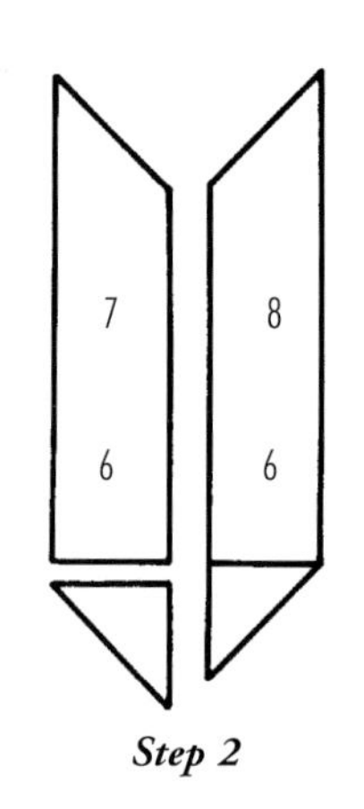

Step 2

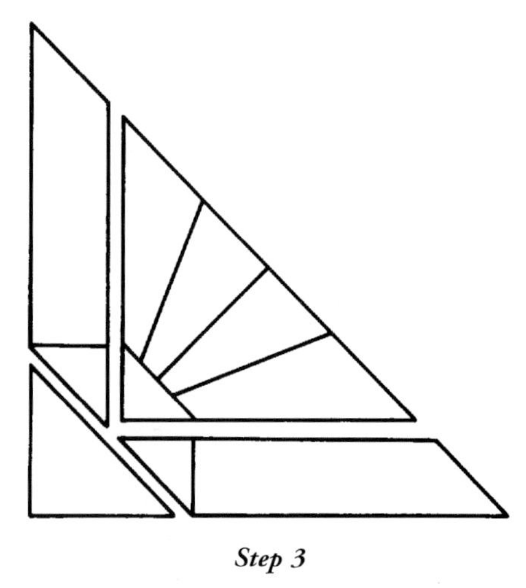

Step 3

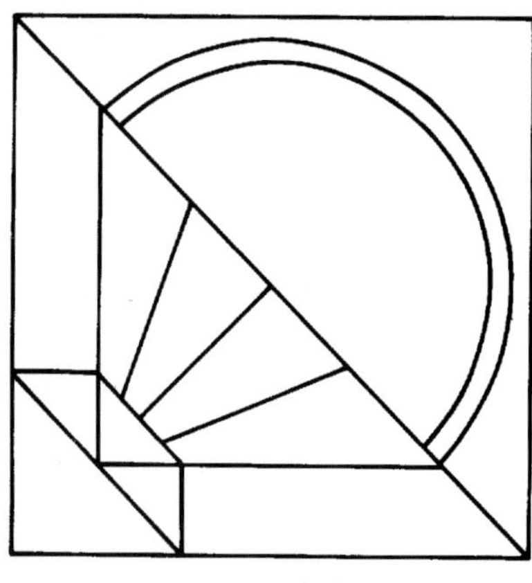

Step 4

- Four strips ⅞in wide on the diagonal for basket handles

From the mauve fabric:

- 4 petals

BLOCK CONSTRUCTION

Using the photograph as a guide, arrange all the basket pieces on a flat surface, following the layout diagram on the pattern sheet. Stitch 1 to 2 and 3 to 4, then stitch 2 to 3. Press all seams towards the darker fabric. Then stitch on 5. Repeat for the remaining three baskets. See Step 1.

Lay the baskets on a flat surface again and place the cream pattern pieces 7 and 8 on either side of the basket. Make sure the angles at the top are facing the right way. Place pattern pieces 6 underneath the straight edge, again making sure the angles are facing the right way and stitch. See Step 2 for basket sides.

Stitch the two units made above to each side of the basket base. Make sure the angles are facing the right way.

Then stitch the cream triangle, pattern 9, to the base. See Step 3.

MAKING THE BASKET HANDLES

Fold each strip of purple fabric into three with the middle division slightly wider than the outer divisions. Fold one side into the middle and tack on the fold to hold in place. Fold the other side down making sure the raw edge does not appear past the first fold. Tack down.

This bias strip will give you a flatter appearance, also having the added advantage of being able to pin it into position before stitching. See Diagram 1.

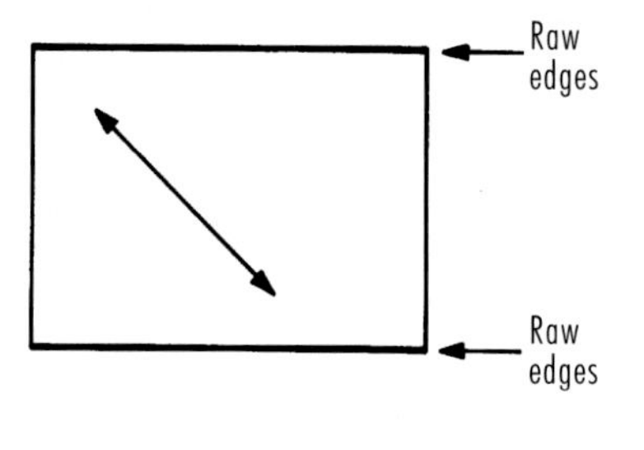

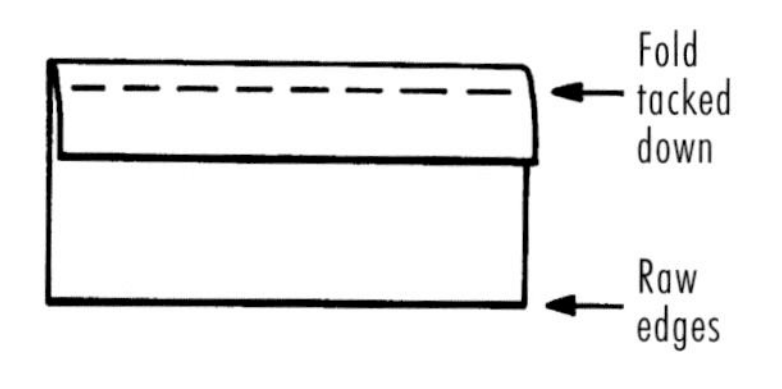

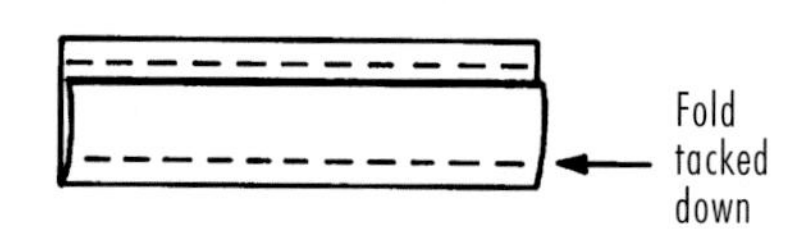

Making the basket handles

ATTACHING THE HANDLE

After making up the handles, tack each one to a pattern piece 10 using the curved template provided on the pattern sheet as a guide.

Stitch the basket block together, then appliqué the handle to the background fabric.

There is another way you can put the handles in if this sounds difficult. Assemble the block, then pin the bias strip into position and tuck the ends under and stitch them even with the seamline instead of securing the ends in the seam.

Note: When stitching on a curved line always stitch the concave (inside of the circle) side first. This will prevent any tucks or pleats. After doing this, you can stitch the convex side (outer side of the circle).

The block should now measure 6 ½in square. Trim if slightly larger.

Make up all four basket blocks, two in each colourway. See Step 4.

CUTTING BORDERS AND SASHINGS

Borders and sashings need to be cut from the remaining fabrics to complete the quilt.

From the blue fabric:

- 2, 1in x 19¾in (top and bottom first border)
- 2, 1in x 20¾in (left and right first border)
- 6, 1in x 6½in sashings
- 4, 1in x 7¾in sashings

From the deep-red fabric:

- 2, 1¾in x 20¾in (top and bottom second border)
- 2, 1¾in x 22¾in (left and right second border)

From the purple fabric:

- 4, 1¾in x 24in strips for binding

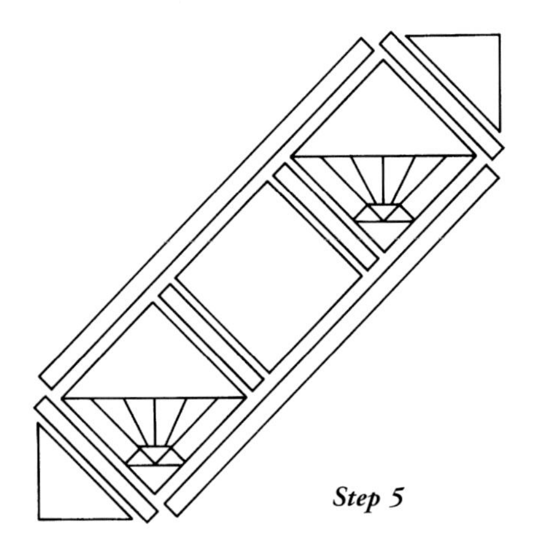

Step 5

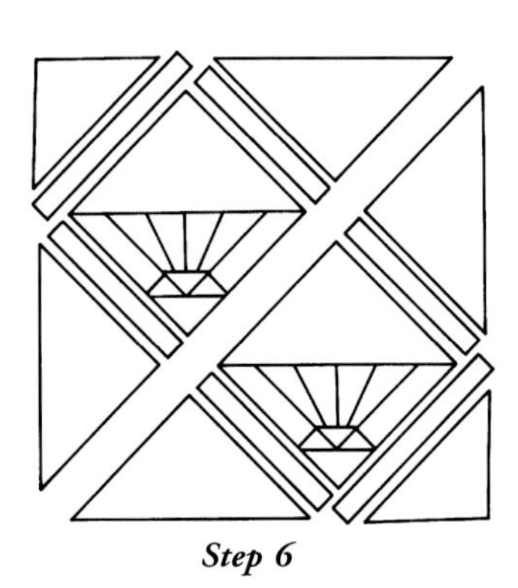

Step 6

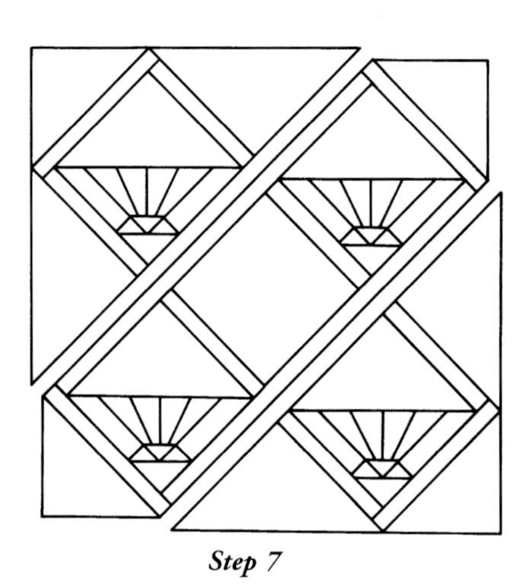

Step 7

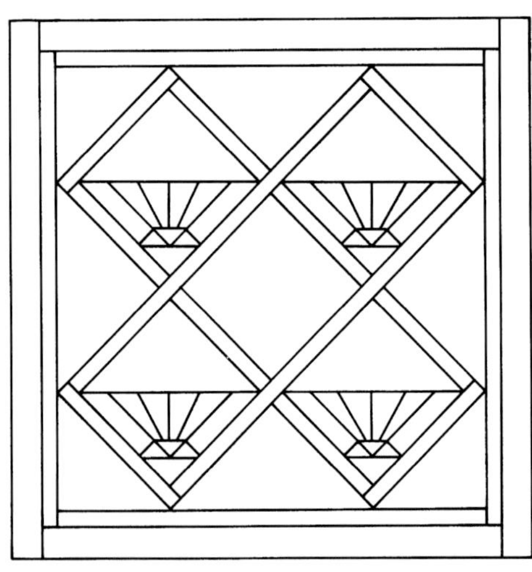

Step 8

APPLIQUE PREPARATION

The adhesive webbing applique method has been used to complete each block. If you decide to use the turn-under method, you will need to add a seam allowance to the appliqué pieces.

Trace 24 petal shapes and 16 leaves onto the smooth side of the adhesive webbing. Roughly cut around each shape. Place the rough side (adhesive side) to the wrong side of the fabric, iron to secure, then cut along the traced line. You will need four mauve, four blue, eight mid red and eight deep red petals. There are two colourways – blue, mid red, deep red; and mauve, mid red, deep red petals. Refer to the photograph for the positioning.

ASSEMBLING THE QUILT TOP

Arrange the baskets with the same colourway and appliqué block 'on point' as shown in Step 5.

Start by stitching a 6½in blue sashing between the lower left block and the appliqué block. Next, sew a sashing to the other side of the appliqué block and then add the upper right block to the row.

Stitch a 19½in sashing along the top and bottom of the strip of three blocks and a 7½in sashing to either end of the strip.

Stitch a corner triangle to either end to complete the strip. See Step 5.

Prepare the top left and bottom right corners by arranging the baskets with the same colorway 'on point' as shown in Step 6. First, stitch a 6½in sashing to either side of the blocks as indicated, then stitch a 7½in sashing to the outer corner sections of the blocks.

Next, stitch filler triangles to the 6½in sashings, then stitch corner filler triangles to the 7½in sashing to complete the corners.

Lining up the sashings, stitch the corner units made previously to either side of the strip unit as shown in Step 7.

Trim the completed quilt top to a 19¾in square.

Borders: Stitch the 1in x 19¾in first border on the top and bottom edges, then stitch the 1in x 20¾in border to the left and right edges.

Stitch the 1½in x 20¾in second border on the top and bottom edges, then stitch the 1½in x 22¾in border to the left and right edges. See Step 8.

Appliqué Motifs: Arrange the prepared flowers and leaves as in the diagram on the pattern sheet, peel off the backing paper and iron into place.

Buttonhole-stitch around each flower in matching embroidery thread. Follow the appliqué block layout for additional embroidery ideas. Use six strands of embroidery thread for running stitch.

When all the embroidery is finished, press from the back. The quilt top is now ready for basting.

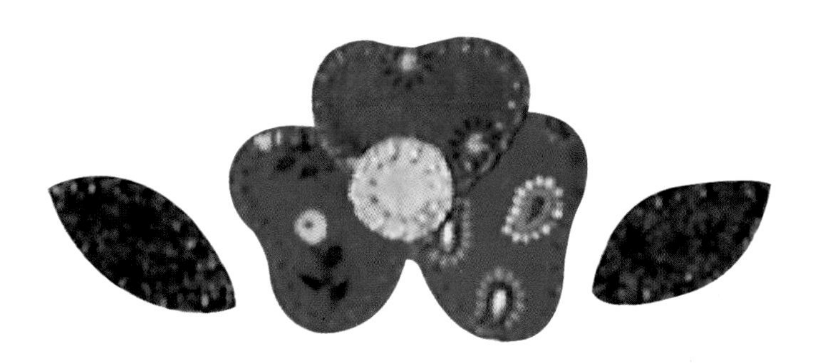

BASTING THE QUILT

Lay the pressed backing fabric right side down on a large surface. Place the wadding evenly onto the wrong side of the backing fabric. Make sure there are no creases in either fabric. Tape the edges of the backing fabric down with masking tape. This will ensure no tucks or creases will appear in the back of the quilt after basting. Place the quilt top wrong side down onto wadding.

Once all three layers are straight, either safety-pin or tack the three layers together so you can quilt.

QUILTING THE DESIGN

Look at magazines or quilting books for inspiration. You can quilt ¼in away from the seam outlining the basket and appliqué designs, or if you prefer to machine quilt, a combination of stippling and grid quilting (as done with this quilt) gives a nice effect. Trim back the batting and backing even with the quilt top.

BINDING

Fold the binding in half lengthwise and press on the folded line.

Pin the raw edges of the binding to the raw edges on the front of the quilt. Stitch using a scant ¼in seam, starting at the top and bottom edges. Trim the excess binding neat with the raw edges on the left and right-hand sides.

Turn the folded edge to the back and pin securely. Repeat on the left and right sides of the quilt, leaving approximately ½in of the binding extended at the beginning and at the other end. Turn under to neaten off the corners and pin. Turn the folded edge to the back and Slip-stitch all the bindings into place onto the backing fabric.

Date and sign your quilt. ❇

1890s Scrap Quilt

While travelling in America, Julie Wallace fell in love with the 1890s scrap quilts she saw. Fuelled with inspiration, she returned home and created this delightful scrap quilt, reminiscent of the colours and patterns of the quilts from this elegant era.

CONSTRUCTION

Take one, 2in x 45in light fabric strip and one, 2in x 45in dark fabric strip. Cut each strip into three equal lengths. These strips will be joined to form two different sets of strip units, each strip unit consisting of three strips. Refer to the photograph on page 66 for the sequence of joining the strips.

Press each strip unit carefully, ensuring the seam allowances are pressed towards the darker colour. Try not to distort the long seam. Cut these strips into 2in strips, cutting across the seams.

The 2in strips will be used for the construction of the two different combinations of the nine-patch blocks as illustrated in the photograph on page 66 and nine-patch blocks diagram below.

Continue joining strips and constructing the nine-patch blocks until you have 143 nine-patch blocks.

TRIANGLE BLOCKS

Take the 5¾in tan strips and cut into 5¾in squares. Next, cut the squares from corner to corner to make half-square triangles. Cut the 5¾in smoky-blue strips in the same manner. Chain-piece a blue half-triangle to a tan half-triangle, right sides together, sewing a ¼in seam along the longest raw edge. Sew all the blue and tan half-triangles together. Press the seam allowance towards the darker fabric.

Next, cut each of the blue and tan triangles from corner to corner, across the fabrics and seam, resulting in two triangles which are half blue and half tan. Place the two pieces together and sew a 1/4in seam to form a block as illustrated in the photograph on page 66. Continue until you have 142 triangle blocks.

ASSEMBLING THE QUILT TOP

The blocks of the quilt are sewn in 19 horizontal rows of 15 blocks. The first row commences with a nine-patch block followed by a triangle block and then another nine-patch block and so on until there is a row of 15 blocks ending with a nine-patch block. Alternate rows commence with a triangle block followed by a nine-patch block. Continue constructing 15 block rows until you have 19 rows in total – 10 rows that begin and end with a nine-patch block and the remaining nine rows that begin and end with a triangle block.

Sew the rows together. Each alternate row should begin with a triangle block. Press all the seams.

Nine-patch block combinations

FINISHED SIZE

- 235cm x 280cm (92in x 110in)

MATERIALS

- 136, 5cm x 115cm (2in x 45in) strips of assorted light fabrics
- 36, 5cm x 115cm (2in x 45in) strips of assorted dark fabrics (Julie recommends using tone-on-tone or small print fabrics rather than plain prints)
- 11, 14.5cm x 115cm (5¾in x 45in) strips of smoky-blue fabric
- 11, 14.5cm x 115cm (5¾in x 45in) strips of cream or tan fabric
- 9, 6.5cm x 115cm (2½in x 45in) strips of fabric for first border
- 9, 13.5cm x 115cm (5¼in x 45in) strips of fabric for second border
- 10, 15cm x 115cm (6in x 45in) strips of fabric for third border
- 3m x 250cm (3⅓yd x 100in) of batting
- 8.6m (9⅜yd) fabric for quilt batting

NOTE: The quilt is sewn with accurate ¼in seams throughout.

The blue and tan squares are cut and then rejoined to form a blue and tan triangle block which has four colour quarters.

The nine-patch blocks are made from 2in strips cut from the two different strip units.

QUILTING

Sew together sections of backing fabric to create a piece large enough for the quilt top. The backing should be approximately 5in larger than the quilt top on all sides.

Lie the backing fabric, right side down, and place the batting over the fabric and then place the quilt top on the batting, right side up. Baste these three layers together.

You may either hand or machine-quilt, or alternatively take the quilt to a professional continuous quilter.

When the quilting is complete, trim away the excess batting and backing to the edges of the quilt top.

ADDING THE BORDERS

Measure the length of your quilt through the centre and down the sides. Cut two strips the same length as your quilt from the 2½in strips of border fabric. You may need to join two or more strips to make two strips the length of your quilt. Pin and sew a border strip to one side of the quilt. Press the seam allowance away from the quilt top. Repeat for the other side of the quilt.

Next, measure the width of the quilt through the centre and across the top and bottom, including the borders.

Cut and join the remaining strips to make two strips the average width of the quilt. Join the border strips to the top and bottom of the quilt. Press the seam allowance away from the quilt top. Repeat this process for the second 5¼in strip border and the third 6in strip border.

BINDING THE QUILT

From the remaining backing fabric, cut 3in strips from selvedge to selvedge. Join the binding strips to make one long strip and iron in half along the length, wrong sides together.

Machine-sew the binding to the quilt top. Starting at the centre bottom and with raw edges together, place the binding strip ½in from the edge of the quilt top. To mitre the border, stop ½in from the corner, backstitch and take out of the sewing machine.

Fold the binding up, making a 45-degree angle with the binding strip. Fold down, level with the edge and sew to the next corner.

Repeat and overlap the ends of the binding. Fold the binding to the back of the quilt and slip-stitch in place, catching the machine stitching and the folded edge of the binding.

Your quilt is now ready for use. Don't forget to date and sign your quilt. ❃

Cosy Country Quilts

All quilts courtesy of Susan Cooper, Marcia Haipo and Kathryn Haipo of Morningside Arts and Crafts (02) 4998 8327.

A Patch of Flowers

Add a floral atmosphere to your dining room with this simply constructed patchwork tablecloth using bright, contemporary fabrics. Designed by Billie Armstrong, this cloth is an achievable challenge for a new patchwork enthusiast, and a quick project for the experienced patchworker.

FINISHED SIZE

- 40in (1m approx) square

MATERIALS

- 150cm (½yd) small floral fabric
- 15cm (⅛yd) large floral fabric
- 15cm (⅛yd) stripe print fabric
- 50cm (½yd) dark blue print fabric
- 30cm (⅓yd) small print fabric
- 30cm (⅓yd) plain cream fabric
- 1.2m (1⅜yd) backing fabric
- 30cm (⅓yd) extra dark blue print fabric for binding
- Matching sewing cotton
- General sewing supplies

NOTE: Wash and iron all fabrics before use. Cut all strips across the width of the fabric.

CUTTING

From the small floral fabric:
cut four strips 4½in wide, then crosscut into 32, 4½in squares.
From the large floral print fabric:
cut four, 4½in squares.
From the stripe print fabric:
cut one strip 4½in, then crosscut into eight 4½in squares.
From the dark blue print fabric:
cut three, 4⅞in strips.
From the small print fabric:
cut two, 4⅞in strips.
From the plain cream fabric:
cut two, 4⅞in strips.

CONSTRUCTION

When making squares where two different colour triangles are sewn together, sew them first to prevent stretching. Place two 4⅞in strips (one of each colour required) with right sides together, then mark into 4⅞in squares. Draw diagonal lines through all the squares then, if needed, mark dotted lines for sewing ¼in seams on either side of the diagonal. (If you have established a ¼in seam mark on your sewing machine, this can be used as a guide.) Refer to Diagram 1.

Pin firmly away from the stitching lines and when stitched, cut into squares

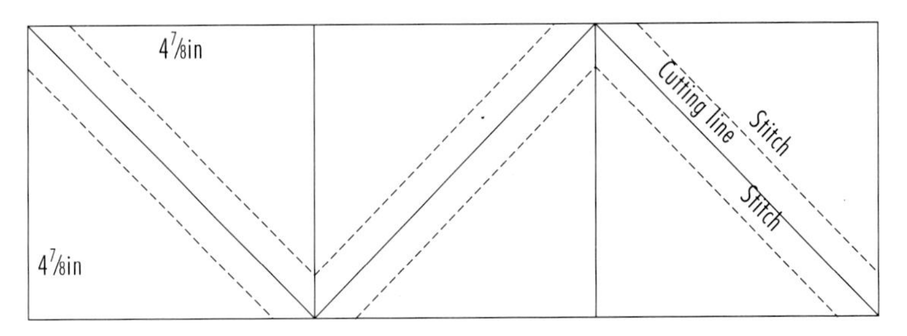

Diagram 1

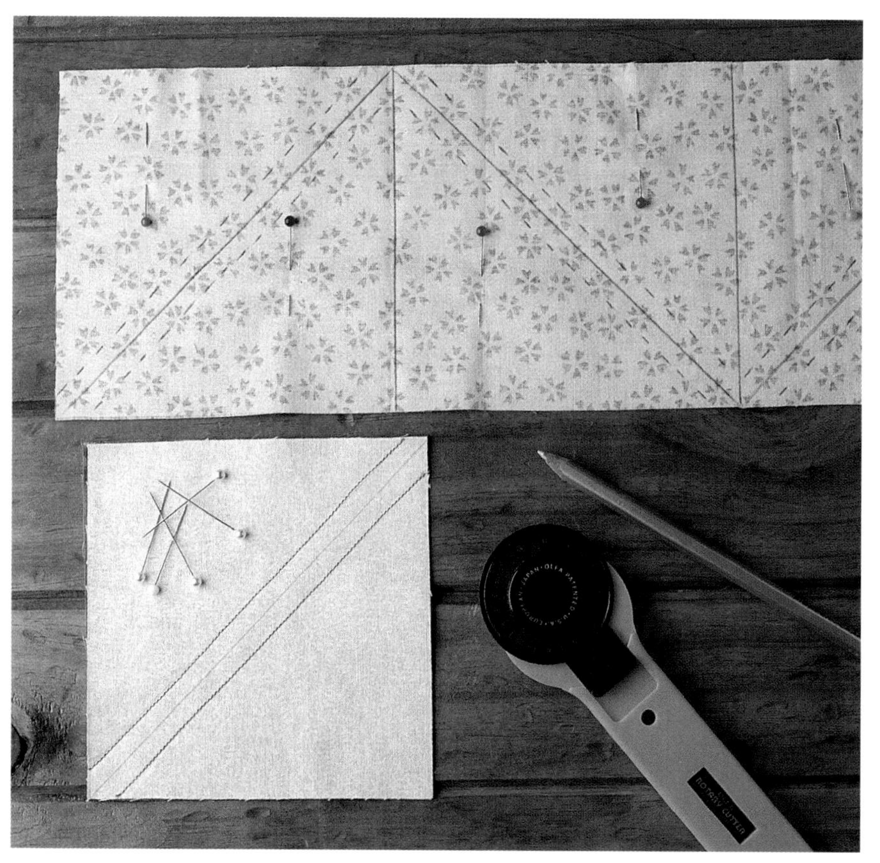

The quick sewing method helps to eliminate stretching the bias seams.

Lay fabric right sides together, matching the seamlines.

then into triangles. Open the triangles, finger-press first avoiding any stretching, then press open. Check you have a 4½in square.

You will need to cut these 4½in squares from the following fabrics:

Dark Blue and Cream: Placing the right sides of the strips together, mark 12 squares. (This will yield 24 squares when cut and opened.)

Cream and Small Print: Placing rights sides of the strips together, mark four squares. (This will yield eight squares.)

Dark Blue and Small Print: Placing right sides of the strips together, mark 12 squares. (This will yield 24 squares.)

Carefully press all squares open making sure you don't stretch the seam. Check that each square measures 4½in.

ASSEMBLY

Lay all the squares out on a flat surface. See the photograph for arrangement of the squares. Sew the squares together using a ¼in seam to form 10 rows. Check that each square measures exactly 4in. Accuracy is very important at this stage.

Cut the backing fabric at least 4in larger than the finished top measurement. (Measure after washing as shrinkage can occur.) Place the first row of squares across the top of the backing fabric approximately 1½in in from the edge. Make sure the backing fabric is very square. Pin in place.

Lay the second row of squares with right sides together on top, making sure all seams and corners match exactly. Sew a ¼in seam across on the lower edge joining together all three layers.

Fold down row two and press carefully. Repeat this method until all the rows have been joined to the backing fabric. If you need to make adjustments to seams or corners now is the time to do it.

BINDING

Trim the edges of the quilt. Cut four strips 1¾in wide from the dark blue binding fabric. Cut the selvedges off. Prepare the binding by sewing the strips into a continuous strip and ironing in half lengthwise, wrong sides together.

Starting at the centre bottom, leave 3in of binding unstitched. Sew onto the front of the quilt top, with all raw edges together, ¼in in from the edge. To mitre the corners, stop ¼in from the corner, backstitch and take the quilt out of the machine. Fold the binding up, making a 45-degree angle, then fold the binding down level with the edge of the quilt. Pin the binding in place and sew along the edge to the next corner and repeat. Finish stitching 3in from the joining point. Join the binding together with a ¼in seam on the wrong side of the fabric, refold and stitch to the cloth. Turn the binding to the back of the quilt and firmly slip-stitch in place. ❁

Friendship Quilt

In the true tradition of both friendship and scrap quilts, Piecemakers designed this cosy quilt using a large variety of scrap fabrics and two different-sized triangular templates.

Note: This quilt is made up of 32 full blocks, 14 half blocks and four quarter blocks.

When selecting your fabrics, if you are using a dark fabric for the D triangles, then consider using lighter fabrics for the C triangles and then darker shades again for the A and B triangles.

The E triangle in each block is the Friendship Panel and made from plain homespun so that a message can be written on it easily. See Diagram 1.

PREPARATION

Cut out plastic templates from the patterns shown on the pattern sheet for the A/B/C template and the D/E template.

The templates should be cut to the sewing line and then an extra ¼in should be added before the fabric shapes are cut out.

Place the templates onto the chosen fabrics, paying particular attention to the straight of the grain.

Use a sharp pencil to draw around the templates, placing a pencil dot at all of the corners. This becomes the sewing line.

Place your quilter's ¼in ruler on the line and draw another line parallel with the first. This becomes our cutting line, giving you a ¼in seam allowance.

CUTTING

From your chosen fabrics cut out four of triangle D, one of E, one of A, one of B, and four of C for each full block. After cutting the triangles for each block you will have 32 A, 32 B, 128 C, 128 D and 32 E triangles.

For each half block cut out one of D, four of C and one of E and for each corner block, four of C. You should have 56 C triangles, 14 D and 14 E and for the corner blocks 16 C. Refer to the block diagrams for guidance.

In the end, you should have 32 A, 32 B, 200 C, 142 D and 46 E triangles.

FINISHED SIZE

- 155cm x 190cm (61in x 75in)

MATERIALS

- Approximately 90, 15cm (6in) squares of printed fabric
- Approximately 24, 10cm (4in) squares of printed fabric
- 30cm (⅓yd) plain homespun for blocks
- 50cm (⅔yd) plain homespun for borders
- 2m (2¼yd) burgundy print fabric for sashings and borders
- 3m (3⅓yd) backing fabric
- Single bed size batting
- Light and dark blending threads to sew all colours
- Quilting thread
- Template plastic
- Pencil
- Sewing machine and general sewing supplies

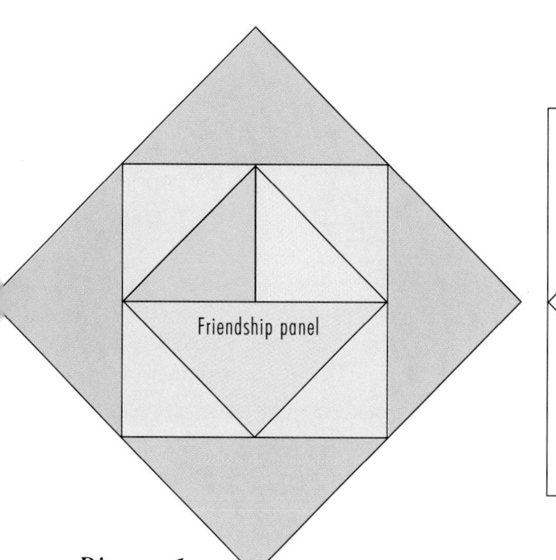

Diagram 1
Make 32 full blocks

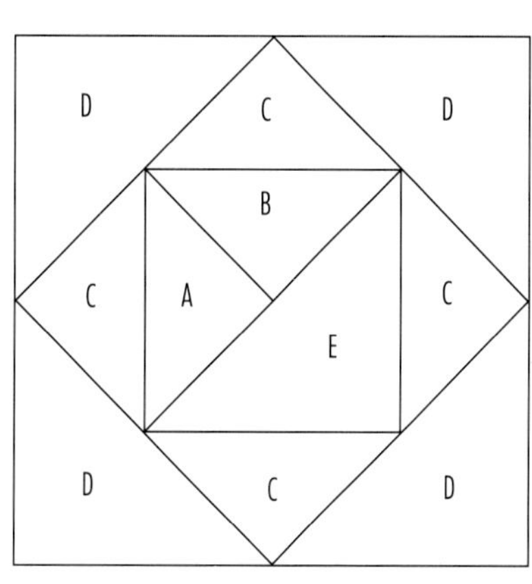

Diagram 2

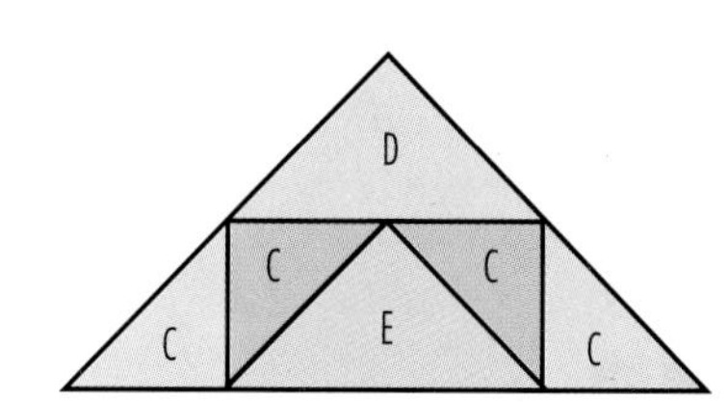

Diagram 3
Make 14 half blocks for edges. Cut 1 D, 1 E and 4 C shapes.

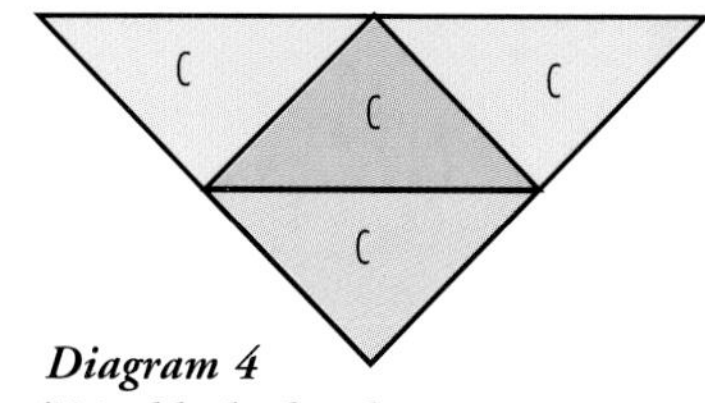

Diagram 4
Make 4¼in blocks for the corners. Cut 4 C shapes.

PIECING THE BLOCKS

Assemble each full block by joining the A and B triangles, then add an E triangle. Attach a C triangle to each side and then a D triangle to each to complete the block. Refer to Diagram 2.

For the half blocks, join a C triangle to each short side of an E triangle. Then add an extra C to each side and then add the D triangle. Refer to Diagram 3.

For the corner triangles, join the four C triangles as shown in Diagram 4.

ASSEMBLY OF THE CENTRAL PANEL

Cut strips of sashing fabric 2½in wide. This will give a finished width of 2in when a ¼in seam allowance is used.

Following the layout diagram on the pattern sheet, join the blocks together in rows with short borders. Then join the rows together to make the central panel of the quilt using the joined lengths and adding half and corner blocks.

ASSEMBLY

To finish the front panel, three borders are added to the outside edge. Cut strips 2½in wide for the first border from the burgundy fabric. Cut strips 1½in wide from plain homespun for the second border and from the remaining burgundy print fabric, 4in wide strips for the final border. Add the side lengths of each border first, then the top and bottom lengths.

QUILTING

Remove the selvedges from the backing fabric, cut it in half and rejoin along the long sides.

Sandwich the backing fabric, batting and quilt top and baste or pin ready for quilting. Hand-quilt around the edge of each shape ¼in from the sewing line.

BINDING

Cut the binding strips 2in wide and join into one length long enough to go around the quilt. Iron the binding in half lengthwise. Place all raw edges together and stitch to the front of the quilt through all thicknesses, leaving a flap for finishing and mitring the corners. Turn the binding to the back and slip-stitch in place.

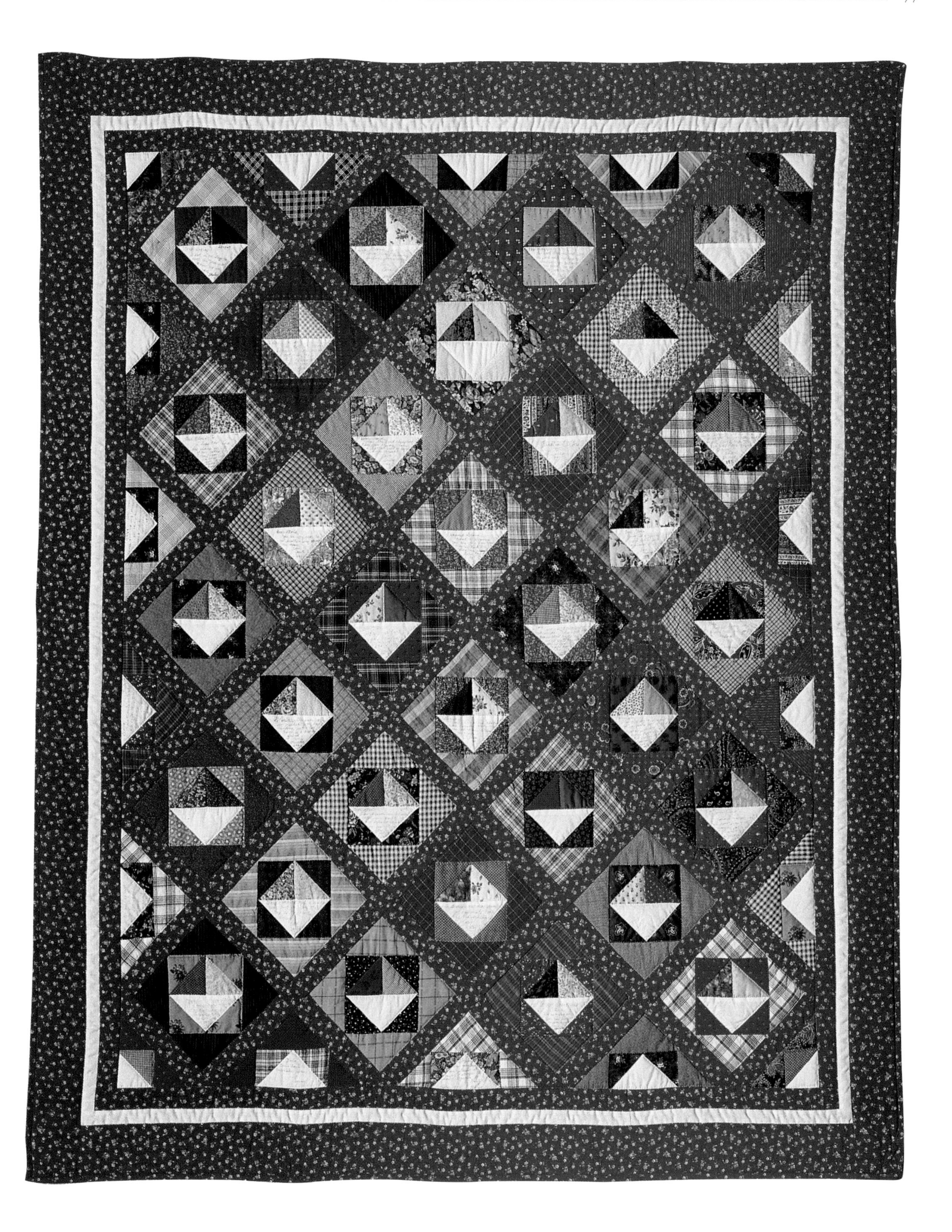

Home Sweet Home

There is no place like home and this appliqué design will let visitors know just how you feel about your humble abode. This classic country design by Deb Thompson can be framed, used as a wall-hanging or a centre panel in a cushion.

INSTRUCTIONS

Using the grey-lead pencil, trace around the design template pieces from the pattern sheet onto a plain sheet of paper and cut them out carefully.

FINISHED SIZE

- Approximately 30cm x 23cm (12in x 9in)

MATERIALS

- 40cm x 30cm (16in x 12in) piece of finely woven calico or homespun
- 20cm (¼yd) double-sided fusible webbing
- Scraps of fabric of your choice plus a small piece of calico or homespun for sign
- Black embroidery cotton
- Black felt-tipped pen
- Fine permanent marking pen
- No 7 or 8 embroidery needle
- Sharp scissors
- Sharp, grey-lead pencil

STITCHES USED

Blanket Stitch, Running Stitch, Long Stitch

TRANSFERRING THE DESIGN

Trace around these template shapes onto the paper side of the double-sided fusible webbing, cutting them out approximately 1cm (⅜in) beyond the pencil line. See Step 1.

Decide which of your fabrics are to be used for each shape – roof, windows, sign etc – and iron the appropriate double-sided fusible webbing shapes, rough side down, onto the back of your chosen fabrics with a dry iron. Take note that one of the 'sign end' pieces must be traced in reverse.

Turn your fabric pieces over and iron again on the reverse side to ensure the webbing has adhered well.

***Step 1** Trace around the template shapes onto the paper side of the double-sided fusible webbing, cutting them out approximately 1cm (⅜in) beyond the pencil line.*

Step 2 Turn over a small 3mm (⅛in) allowance edge and stitch a small continuous running stitch through this edge and around the entire outer edge of the circle.

LAYING OUT THE DESIGN

Cut out your fabric fused shapes on the pencil line with sharp scissors, ensuring a crisp edge. Peel the backing paper from the pieces and place the house and roof pieces, gently butting together, onto the calico background fabric. Using a dry iron, carefully iron the pieces into place. Do not have your iron on a very hot setting or the calico background fabric will scorch. An ironing cloth or another piece of calico placed over the pieces while ironing helps prevent this. Continue the placement and ironing of the door, windows, mat, leaves and trees. Turn fabric over and iron again on the back. Place the coloured fabric arch over the house, making sure it is level. Underlap the two end sections of the sign before ironing them in place. See Step 3.

Step 3 Peel the paper backing from the pieces, place the house and roof pieces, butting together, onto the calico background fabric. Using a dry iron, iron pieces into place.

HOME SWEET HOME SIGN

Write the Home Sweet Home wording onto the calico section of the sign before ironing it in place. To do this, trace over the wording on the pattern sheet on a plain sheet of paper with a black felt-tipped pen and tape it onto a flat surface. Lay a scrap of calico over the words and, using the permanent marking pen, practise writing on this before moving onto the sign. Sufficient lettering can be seen through the fabric to use it as a guide for your writing. (Writing words onto the sign once it is ironed means if you make a mistake it is there to stay! If you are unhappy with your first attempt, try again until you're satisfied with the way it looks.) Lay the calico sign onto the coloured sign ensuring it is level, then iron into place.

SUFFOLK PUFF FLOWERS

The fabric for the Suffolk puff flowers should not be fused with webbing. With the wrong side of the fabric facing, turn over a small 3mm (1/8in) allowance edge and stitch a small continuous running stitch through this edge around the entire outer edge of the circle. Pull the thread gently but firmly and the circle will gather in on itself, turning the correct side of the fabric to the centre. See Step 2. Press down with your fingers until it sits flat. Sew the flowers in place while the thread is still attached.

FINISHING

To finish the design, use a single strand of black embroidery thread and Blanket-stitch around the fabric edges. Deb worked a small Running Stitch around the leaves and the tree trunks. This stitch can be used in place of the Blanket Stitch on any of the fabric pieces. Using two strands of thread to work long stitches for the window panes and two strands of thread to work Running Stitch for the flower stems. Refer to the photograph.

The design is now complete and ready to be framed or bound as you desire. ❄

Country Harvest Scarecrow

Inspired by a painted design by Bev Stacey, Christine Book has used textiles and easy appliqué techniques to create this delightful country-style cushion.

Note: Please read all instructions before commencing work. All fabrics should be 100 per cent cotton, washed and ironed. A 6mm (1/4in) seam allowance is used throughout and included in the cutting instructions.

APPLIQUE

All the applique shapes on this cushion are completed using quick, fusible techniques. Study the appliqué design on the pattern sheet and select your fabrics for each element of the design.

The pattern for this design has been reversed. This ensures that the shapes will be fused on the correct way after tracing them onto the paper side of the fusible webbing.

Using a lead pencil, trace each of the shapes from the design onto the paper side of the double-sided fusible webbing. It is a good idea to label each shape with its name and number – this will help identify them when it comes to assembling the design.

Once the shapes are all traced, roughly cut out each one. Now place the rough, or glue, side of the fusible webbing onto the wrong side of your chosen fabric and using a hot iron, press into position.

Using sharp scissors, carefully cut around each pencil line and peel off the backing paper. Position your pieces onto the osnaburg, using the numbering sequence on the pattern and the photograph as a guide.

Some pieces underlap other pieces, so take care when placing fabric. When all the shapes are in position, carefully press them in place.

Be sure to apply enough heat to dissolve the glue and adhere all shapes in place securely.

FINISHED SIZE

- 71cm x 56cm (28in x 22in)

MATERIALS

- 50cm x 35cm (20in x 14in) seeded osnaburg for background
- 50cm (½yd) yellow wheat fabric
- 30cm (⅓yd) of red and orange corn-print fabric
- 60cm (⅝yd) of iron-on Pellon wadding
- 60cm (⅝yd) fabric for cushion back
- Assorted scraps of print fabrics for appliqué
- DMC Coton Perlé No 3: dark topaz (782)
- DMC Coton Perlé No 5: medium mahogany (301) and other colours slightly darker than your appliqué fabrics
- DMC Coton Perlé No 8: medium brown (433)
- 30cm (⅓yd) double-sided fusible webbing
- Two small black buttons
- Two small mustard buttons
- Four large buttons for corners of panel
- Brown permanent marking pen
- Fine, permanent black marker
- Approximately 73cm x 46cm (29in x 18in) large cushion insert
- No 7 or 8 embroidery needle
- Lead pencil
- General sewing supplies

STITCHES USED

Whipped Chain Stitch, Blanket Stitch, Backstitch, Running Stitch, French Knot, Straight Stitch

EMBROIDERY

An embroidery needle is used throughout except for the scarecrow's straw. The straw requires a chenille needle to accommodate the thicker Perlé No 3 thread.

Outline the leaves in Blanket Stitch, with the veins Backstitched in a paler green. The pumpkins and gourd and their stalks are outlined in Blanket Stitch with the details stitched in Backstitch.

The scarecrow's overalls are outlined in Whipped Chain Stitch. His shirt and braces are stitched in a small, even Backstitch. The front details on the shirt are added with Backstitch and Running Stitch. The patches on the overalls are stitched in place with naive Straight Stitch, Running Stitch and small Cross Stitches.

Trace the scarecrow's straw details from the pattern using the fine permanent marker pen. Backstitch the straw with dark topaz Perlé No 3.

Using matching thread, stitch the scarecrow's face with small, even Blanket Stitches. Draw on the face details using the black permanent marker. Work a white French Knot for the highlight in the eyes. The scarecrow's hat is worked using Blanket Stitch.

When all the stitching has been completed, place your work back over the pattern and trace in the background details. Trace the cornfield and ground details with the brown marking pen. Use the medium brown Perlé No 8 thread to work simple running stitches over the ground and horizon area.

Once all the embroidery details are complete, stitch the black buttons on the shirt front and the mustard buttons in place on the braces. Trim your cushion panel down to measure 47cm x 32cm (18½in x 12½in).

ASSEMBLING THE CUSHION

From the border fabric (wheat print), cut two 47cm x 9cm (18½in x 3½in) strips for the top and the bottom panels, and two 47cm x 9cm (18½in x 3½in) side strips. Stitch these to the centre panel and press the seam allowance towards the border.

From the corn fabric, cut two 62cm x 6cm (24½in x 2½in) strips for the top and the bottom and two 57cm x 6cm (22 ½in x 2½in) strips for the sides.

Machine-stitch these strips to your cushion panel as before and press the seam allowance towards the darker outer fabrics.

Cut out the iron-on Pellon so it is slightly larger than the front panel. With the fabric side up, press the Pellon to the back of the cushion front, using a hot steam iron.

Using the medium mahogany Perlé No 5, work a row of primitive Cross Stitch, with two large running stitches between each cross, as a decorative trim around the centre panel.

To make the cushion backing, cut two 58cm x 42cm (23in x 16½in) pieces of fabric. Machine-stitch a 2.5cm (1in) rolled hem on one long side of each piece. Overlap the two seamed edges until their combined size fits the cushion front.

Pin the overlap in place, then with right sides together, pin the back to the front. Trim back the Pellon and carefully machine-stitch around the cushion. Clip the corners and remove the pins, holding the overlap. Turn right side out.

To create the frill or flange, machine-stitch through both layers of the fabric in the ditch where the corn fabric joins the wheat border.

Insert your pillow filler, slip-stitch the opening closed and sew four large buttons at the corners of the design in the centre of the cushion. ❄

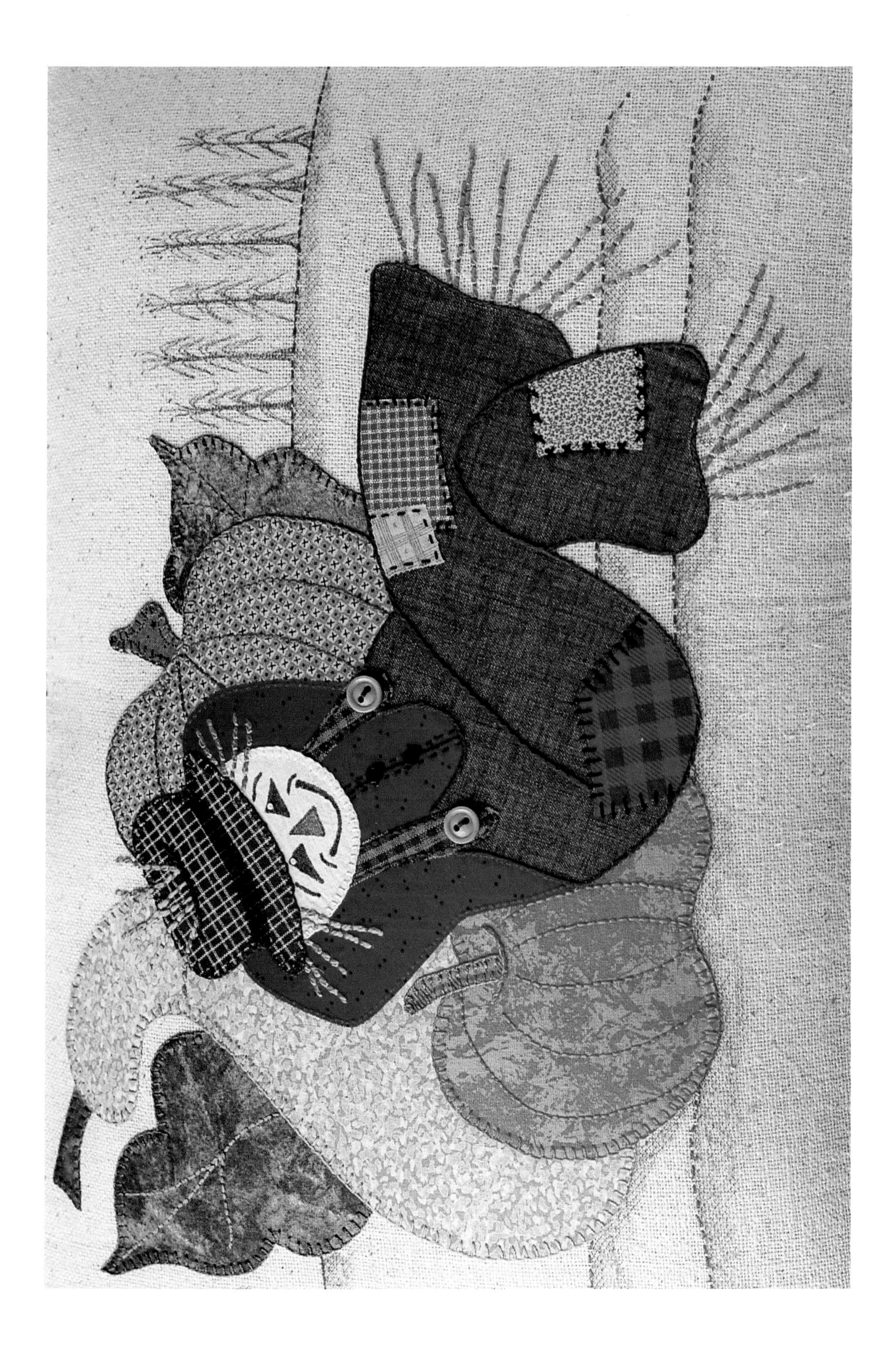

Emily's Flannel Quilt

There's a warm country feel about this delightful flannel quilt made by Tita Leach to complement her daughter Emily's four-poster bed. This quilt can be adapted in size and looks marvellous in checks, florals and solids.

PREPARATION

Using the 6½in Sew Easy Square cut approximately 10 squares from each flannel fabric, giving you a total of 130 squares. Tita cut a few extra of some colours to provide additional fabric choice if needed when placing squares together.

Note: If using checks, try to align the lines of the check with the easy square. A seam allowance of 6mm (¼in) has been included to give a finished square of 6in.

CUTTING

Lay the large sheet down in an open floor space. This will prevent the squares getting dirty while you organise your quilt layout. Once you are satisfied that similar colours are not touching and look evenly scattered, start to join them up. Join one row at a time.

Repeat for all 13 rows. Once these are completed, press the seams open or to one side. Now join the rows. By leaving them on the sheet in their rows until you actually come to stitch them, you will prevent mistakes in placement.

Once all 130 squares are connected, hearts can be placed at random over the quilt. Choose as many as you prefer and in any size. Tita used 11 small and 15 large hearts, even the reverse side of the flannel can be used. See the photograph for placement.

Using a pencil, trace enough large and small hearts from the pattern sheet onto the smooth side of the double-sided fusible webbing. Cut out leaving a 6mm (¼in) margin around each heart. Choose several contrasting flannel colours. Iron the heart shapes onto the back of the fabric. Cut out on the pencil line. Again, position the hearts at random on top of the quilt maintaining a good balance. Once you are finally satisfied with regard to positioning, pin the hearts in place to hold while you iron on the shape, remembering to peel off the backing paper first.

EMBROIDERY

Using a flower thread to contrast with your fabric, Buttonhole-stitch around the edge of each heart. Do not Blanket-stitch as this will not secure the hearts firmly.

QUILTING

Make up the quilt by laying backing fabric, wadding and the finished quilt panel into a sandwich. Depending on the size of the quilt you may need to join both the backing fabric and the wadding. Before cutting out, work out which is the most economical way. Remember to leave at least 12cm (5in) extra of wadding and backing protruding from under your quilt panel. This excess will support the binding. Firmly tack these three layers in place using a large zigzag stitch.

ASSEMBLY

The wooden buttons can be either sewn on now, or at the completion of the binding.

To place and stitch on the buttons, start at the centre of the quilt. Then work around this button placing one on each side and then above and below. This is very important to prevent puckering. Repeat until all the buttons have been

FINISHED SIZE

- 13 x 10 squares

BLOCK SIZE

- 15cm (6in)

MATERIALS

SINGLE BED SIZE

- 35cm (⅓yd) of 13 flannel fabrics
- 3.5m (4yd) backing fabric
- 2.5m (2¾yd) binding fabric
- 3.5m (4yd) batting
- Wooden buttons (single bed quilt requires 108)
- 3 packets Ginny Thompson Flower Thread to complement overall colour scheme
- Sew Easy Square, 6½in for accurate cutting
- 50cm (20in) double-sided fusible webbing
- Pencil
- Rotary cutter and board
- Large flat bed sheet, for planning placement of squares

STITCHES USED

Buttonhole Stitch

NOTE: It is essential to pre-wash all fabric, except the batting, before use. Wash in warm water, rinse well, dry naturally and press when dry.
The following instructions are for a single bed sized quilt.

stitched through all three layers on the join where each square meets. This holds the quilt together so that no quilting is required.

BINDING

Divide the binding fabric into eight 45cm (18in) strips across the fabric. If you want a narrower binding, cut the strips accordingly.

Join two strips together to form four very long strips. Fold the binding in half lengthwise, iron and iron in half again then attach to the quilt. Place and pin the top and bottom bindings first. Machine in place with 1cm (½in) seam. Trim back excess wadding and backing to 8cm (3¼in) from the machine line. Fold the binding over towards the underside of the quilt and slip-stitch into position.

Repeat for the side bindings, but leave at least 8cm (3¼in) at either end of the binding strips. Pin, then stitch in place. Trim back to 8cm (3¼in) and fold the binding to the back. The extra 8cm (3¼in) is turned under before stitching to give the quilt a nice neat edge. Slip or ladder-stitch the binding into position. ❄

Charm 'n' Country

This delightful naive appliqué wall-hanging by Anne Gleeson is the ideal piece to display on the wall in your country-style kitchen.

PIECED PATCHWORK

From the plain cotton fabric, cut three strips to resemble shelves on the hutch. The first one measures 46cm x 6.5cm (18¼in x 2½in), the second 46cm x 4cm (18¼in x 1 5/8in) and the third 46cm x 2.5cm (18¼in x 3/4in). Place to one side.

Cut two strips from the light print 46cm x 21cm (18in x 8¼in) and 46cm x 19cm (18in x 7½in).

Arrange the print and plain fabric strips in order, starting at the bottom, followed by the largest background strip. Machine-sew the strips together and iron each seam towards the darkest fabric. Place to one side.

From the checked fabric, cut two strips, each measuring 50cm x 5cm (19⅝in x 2in). Pin each strip on either side of the panel you have just sewn and stitch in place. See Diagram 1. Trim away any excess fabric and press.

To create a roof-like effect at the top of the hutch, take the lighter (background) fabric and with the wrong sides facing, fold in half so the straight edges are matching together along the same side. You will need a minimum total width of 54cm (21¼in), or 27cm (10¾in) when the fabric piece is folded. From the straight edge, measure a distance of 17.5cm (7in) along the edge and mark with a pencil. Now take the ruler to the opposite edge of the folded fabric and measure a distance of 6cm (2⅜in) from the straight edge. Rule a pencil line between the two points and cut along the pencil line. You now have the sloped roof of the hutch. See Diagram 2.

Next, fold the checked fabric in half, right sides out, being sure to match the straight edges together along the same side. Measure a distance of 5cm (2in) up from the straight edge along the folded edge of fabric. Go to the opposite edge and measure a distance of 16cm (6¼in). Rule a pencil line between the two marks and cut along this line. See Diagram 3. The two pieces should butt together when opened out on a flat surface.

Find the centre point of each piece and measure in 6mm (¼in) from the raw edge. With right sides together, pin the two pieces together, matching the centres carefully. Machine-stitch together using a 6mm (¼in) seam allowance. Join the top of the hutch to the lower half assembled earlier. Trim off any excess fabric and press the seams flat on the back of the work.

APPLIQUE

Trace each appliqué design from the pattern sheet and put to one side. Select a range of fabric pieces or leftover scraps of material that coordinate with the background of the hutch and with one another. Using a pen, transfer the outline of each template onto the rough side of the fusible webbing and cut out. With the rough side of the double-sided webbing placed on the wrong side of the fabric, iron on a flat surface, using a hot setting. Cut out each piece and put aside until you are ready to decide on the placement of each piece. Choose your own layout if you wish. Peel off the backing paper and iron into place, leaving the doll until last. Blanket-stitch around each piece, using three strands of matching stranded cotton.

For a little more texture, the doll and the flowers in the basket have been treated differently to give them a three-dimensional effect.

Flowers: For the flowers in the basket, cut out three different-sized circles from several different fabric pieces. To make the yoyos (also known as Suffolk puffs) resemble flowers, fold a small hem over to the wrong side of the fabric and work a running stitch around the circle.

FINISHED SIZE

- 70cm x 56cm (28in x 22in)

MATERIALS

- 50cm (⅝yd) each of three contrasting cotton fabrics for country hutch and bindings
- 70cm x 60cm (¾yd x 24in) calico or homespun for backing
- 70cm x 60cm (¾yd x 24in) thin wadding
- Assorted cotton prints suitable for appliqué and yoyos
- 20cm (8in) double-sided fusible webbing
- DMC Stranded Embroidery Cotton: very dark garnet (902), dark Christmas red (498), very dark antique blue (3750), dark blue green (501)
- Matching quilting threads
- No 9 crewel embroidery needle
- No 9 quilting needle
- Template plastic (optional)
- Pencil, water-erasable pen, ruler
- Sewing machine and accessories
- Assorted buttons for flower centres

NOTE: For her contrasting fabrics Anne has selected one plain for the shelving, a light print for the background and a checked fabric for the sides and top of the country hutch.

STITCHES USED

Blanket Stitch, Running Stitch

NOTE: A 6mm (¼in) seam allowance is included in all cutting measurements.

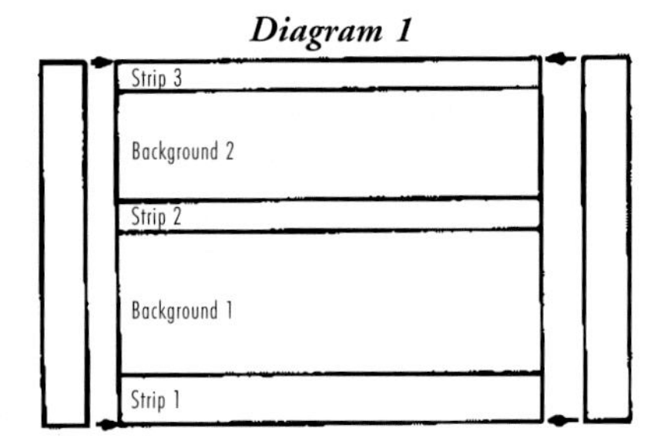

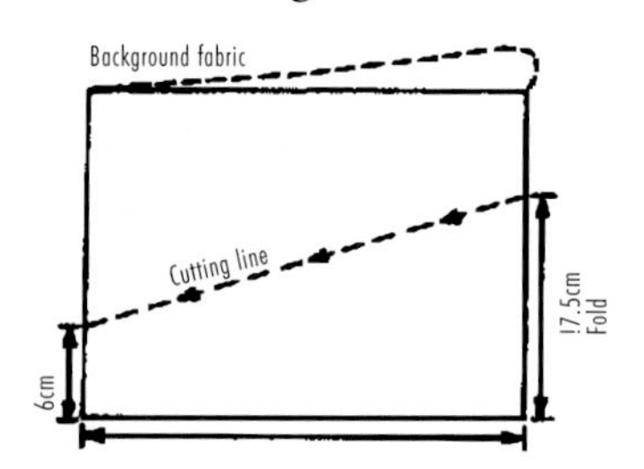

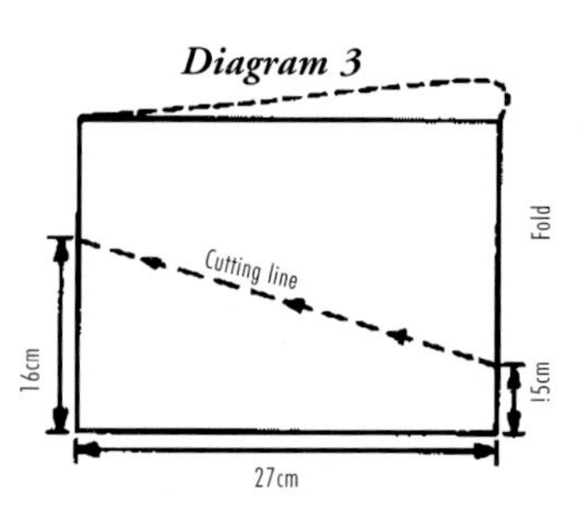

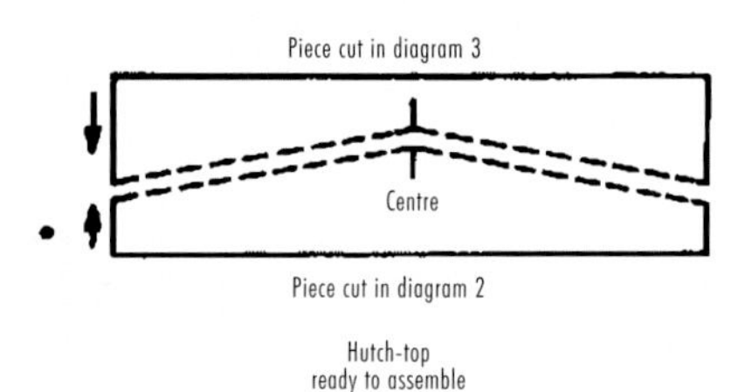

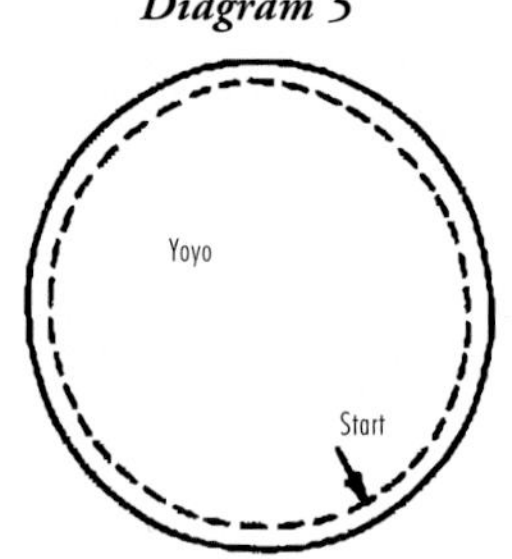

Pull the thread up to gather in the centre of each yoyo. Put some extra flowers on the shelf and anchor with a button in the centre.

Doll: To give the doll a little more life, cut a strip of calico or homespun, measuring 25cm x 5cm (9⅞in x 2in). Fold the strip in half and machine-stitch along the entire length for the arms and the other half to make the two legs.

To make the arms, find the mid-point and complete a single overhand knot, which resembles two clasped hands.

Pin the doll's dress in position and tuck the raw ends of the calico arms under the dress fabric at the point where the shoulders would be. Secure with a couple of backstitches to hold in place.

Cut the second strip (which you put aside earlier) in half to create two short leg lengths. Complete an overhand knot on one end of each strip. Tuck the raw ends under the bottom edge of the dress and stitch securely in place. They may be left to hang loose, or anchored into place with a colourful bow.

Blanket-stitch around the entire dress, then iron the circle in place for the head. Now, Blanket-stitch the circle in place. Embellish the face and hair using three strands of contrasting cotton. Stitch two eyes and a mouth, then randomly stitch around the outside of the circle to resemble hair. Tie each strand of hair with a double overhanded knot to secure in place. See the photograph for detail.

QUILTING AND BINDING

Sandwich a small length of thin wadding between a suitable piece of backing fabric (washed calico or homespun) and the top appliquéd layer. Baste all three layers together to avoid any movement during the quilting process.

Choose your own quilting design to join all layers together, or quilt in straight lines over the background areas, matching the angle of the roof and the straight edges of the pieced area.

Hint: Use a narrow masking tape to achieve straight and evenly-spaced quilting lines.

Cut four strips from any one or more of the three fabrics used in the quilt top, each measuring 6.5cm (2½in) wide. Be sure to allow a little extra length for turning under the folded ends at the hemming stage. Cut one extra strip 5cm (2in) wide for a rod pocket to be stitched on the back.

Fold the first strip in half lengthwise, right side out and align the two raw edges with the raw edge of the quilt front. Machine-sew the first binding strip using a 6mm (¼in) seam allowance. Repeat for the opposite side, leaving the top and bottom seams till last. Trim and neaten all excess fabrics in line with the binding edge.

Turn all four bindings to the back and hem in place. Position a rod sleeve strip, 46cm x 4.6cm (18in x 2½in), at the top on the quilt back and hem by hand, making sure not to go through to the front layer.

Hang on a length of hidden dowel, or use one of the attractive wire hangers available in craft stores, to display your finished quilt. Add a small length of raffia to the ends of the wire for that added country touch. ❆

Sweetheart Crib Quilt

This adorable crib quilt by Pam Deshon is made from a collection of 1930s style fabrics which create a light and pretty effect for your favourite little one.

PREPARATION AND CUTTING

This quilt is made up of nine-patch blocks set 'on point' within squares to give a square-within-a-square appearance. There are two ways to construct the nine-patch blocks. Firstly, you can cut 157 squares, each 1½in x 1½in from the cream fabric, and 158 squares, each 1½in x 1½in from assorted prints.

Sew them to form nine-patch blocks, 18 with four cream squares in each and 17 with five cream squares in each. See Diagram 1. Alternatively, cut strips of fabric 1½in wide and 7in long. If you have 35 different fabrics, you will only need one strip of each. You will also need 54 strips, each 1½in x 7in of cream fabric.

Sew the strips together lengthways into sets of two. See Diagram 2. Cut three, 1½in segments from each strip set and sew into two opposite nine-patch blocks.

CONSTRUCTING THE BLOCKS

The triangles for the corners of the nine-patch on squares blocks are cut from 3½in squares. These are cut in half on the diagonal to give two triangles from each square. If you have 35 colour prints, you will need two squares of each colour.

Altogether, you will need to cut 70 squares which will give you 140 triangles. Sew a triangle to each side of the nine-patch blocks to make a square-within-a-square. Make sure you place a different colour on each side.

CONSTRUCTING THE QUILT

Lay the squares in seven rows with five squares in each row, until you have a pleasing effect. It is preferable not to place two of the same colour side by side.

Sew the square units into rows with five squares in each. Press the seams between square units of rows 1, 3, 5 and 7 to the right and press the seams between square units of rows 2, 4 and 6 to the left. When the rows are sewn together, the seams will butt against each other and hold each other in place. Sew the rows together to form the quilt top.

BORDERS

Cut two strips of cream fabric each 20½in x 2in. Sew one to the top and one to the bottom of the quilt. Cut two strips of cream fabric, each 34in x 2½in. Sew one strip to each side of the quilt.

QUILTING

Place the backing, the wadding and the quilt top together. Pin with safety pins. Machine quilt using a walking foot on your machine or hand-quilt if you prefer.

BINDING

Cut 2in strips of a print to fit each side and the top and bottom of the quilt. Press in half lengthways. Stitch, then trim excess, so there is about ¾in remaining after trimming. Fold the binding to the back of the quilt and slip-stitch in position. Repeat for the sides of the quilt, leaving 1in extra at each end to fold under to neaten the corners. Slip-stitch to the back of the quilt and Ladder-stitch together the corner edges. ❆

FINISHED SIZE

- 62cm x 85cm (25in x 34in)

MATERIALS

- 1.2m (1⅜yd) assorted prints (This quilt used one strip 10cm x 38cm [4in x 15in] of each of 35 different prints)
- 60cm (24in) cream fabric (30cm [12in] for the quilt, 30cm [12in] for the border)
- 25cm (10in) print fabric for the binding
- 60cm (24in) backing fabric
- 70cm x 90cm (28in x 36in) piece of wadding
- Quilting thread
- Cream sewing thread

STITCHES USED

Ladder Stitch

NOTE: Seams of ¼in are used throughout.

All fabrics are 100 per cent cotton and are pre-washed to make them softer and easier to use.

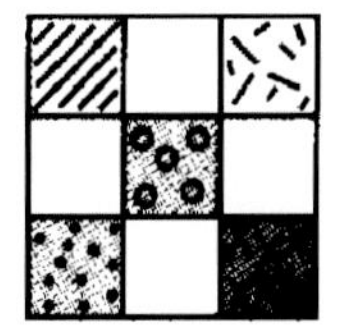
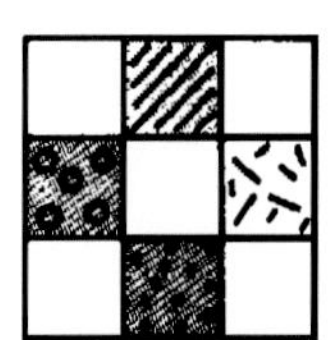

Diagram 1

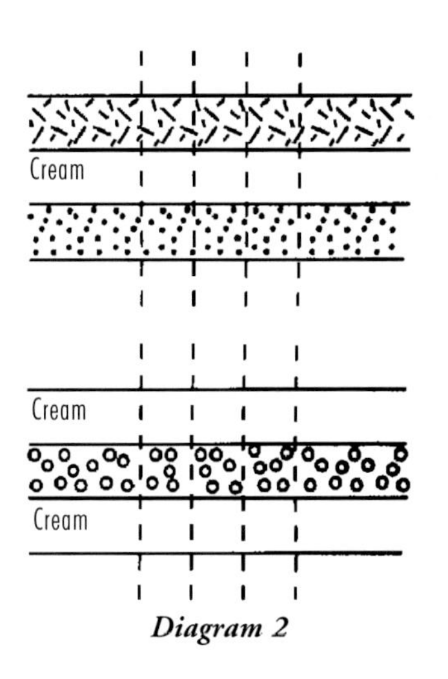

Diagram 2

Lost Ships Quilt

Dusky browns and twilight blues combine in this stunning but simple scrap bag quilt which has ships sailing in giddy diagonals across its surface.

CUTTING

From the background fabric, cut 13 strips, each 2½in wide. Cut each of these strips into 2½in squares. You need seven squares for each block. Draw a diagonal line across each square on the wrong side of the fabric, using a pencil with a fine point.

Also from the background fabric, cut two strips, each 2⅞in wide. Cut these strips into 2⅞in squares. Cut each square diagonally into two triangles. You need two of these triangles for each block.

From each of your selected print fabrics, cut one strip 2½in wide. Cut each strip into 2½in squares. You need seven squares of the same fabric for each block.

ASSEMBLING EACH BLOCK

Place each 2½in print square right sides together with a 2½in background square, matching exactly. Sew from corner to corner following the drawn diagonal line. **HINT:** Sew without cutting the thread between each pair of squares to create a string of seven squares, then cut the squares apart.

Fold one corner of the print fabric back over the other and press. Do not iron, but press firmly. This is to avoid stretching the sewn bias line out of shape and distorting the true square required. Trim away excess fabric ¼in from the sewn line.

From another print fabric, cut one 6⅞in square. Cut the square diagonally to form two medium triangles. Set one aside for another block.

From a third print fabric, cut one 10⅞in square. Cut the square diagonally to form two large triangles. Set one aside for use in another block. Lay out seven sewn bias squares, two 2⅞in background

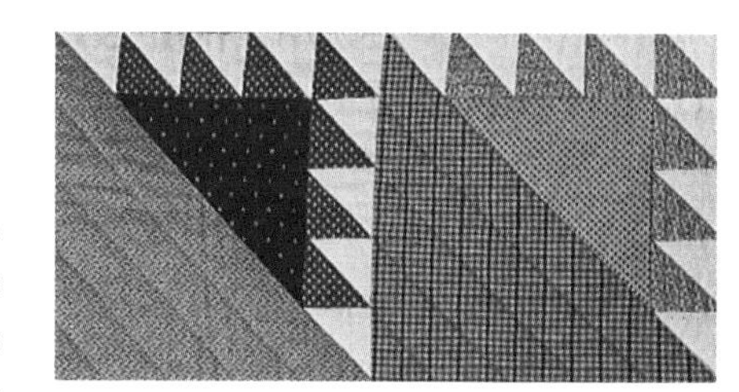

triangles and a medium and a large print triangle to form the block design.

Sew three squares and one light triangle together, matching straight edges. Sew with an exact ¼in seam allowance. Press seams towards the dark triangles.

Sew this section to the side of the medium triangle, matching the straight edges. Press seams under the triangle.

Sew the other four pieced squares and one light triangle together. Press the seams under the dark triangle. Place over the already sewn section, matching the seams with a pin before sewing. Press the seam under the medium triangle. Be careful not to stretch the bias edge when pressing. See Diagram 1.

Lay the pieced section over the large triangle, matching straight outer edges. Sew carefully, ruffling up the bias edge slightly and feeding the fabric into the needle so that no stretching occurs. Press this seam under the large triangle. See Diagram 2.

Check that the finished block measures 10½in. Make 24 more blocks in the same way. Enjoy mixing your fabrics for different effects. Make some blocks light, some dark and some medium.

ASSEMBLING THE QUILT TOP

Join five blocks together in rows, then join rows together to form the central body of the quilt. This quilt has 25 blocks, but the number could be adjusted to make a larger or smaller quilt.

FINISHED SIZE

- 160cm (63in) square

MATERIALS

- 3m (3¼yd) light background fabric such as homespun
- 4m (4⅜yd) in total of assorted print fabrics, 30cm (⅜yd) of each
- 70cm (¾yd) fabric for binding
- 3.5m (3⅞yd) fabric for backing
- 170cm (1⅞yd) square of wadding
- Sewing thread to blend with fabrics
- Sewing machine
- Rotary cutter and mat
- Quilter's ruler showing ⅛in
- Small safety pins
- HB pencil

NOTE: All cutting measurements include a 6mm (¼in) seam allowance.
Forty-six different print fabrics have been used in this quilt.
Fabric amounts are based on 115cm (45in) wide fabric.

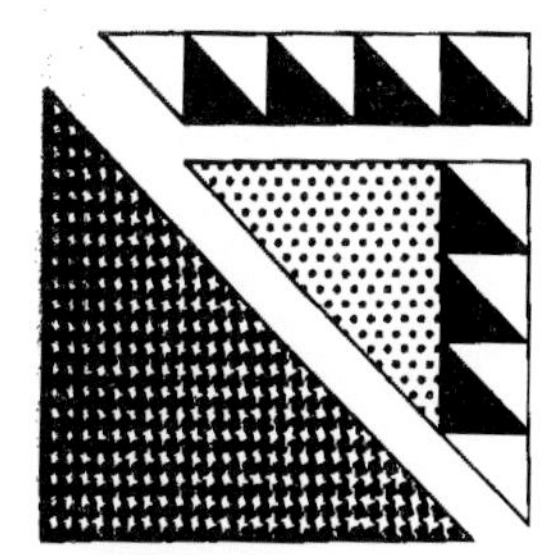

Diagram 1

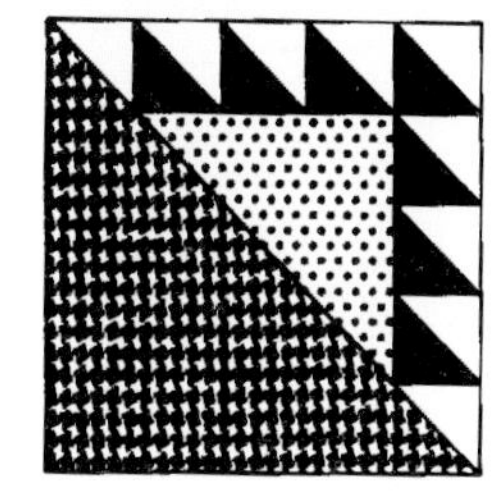

Diagram 2

Join strips made up of bias squares to the medium triangle.

Take care not to stretch the bias edges when sewing the final diagonal seam for each block.

ADDING BORDERS

Cut four borders lengthwise from the remaining light homespun background fabric, each 7in x 62in. Press and trim the quilt edges. Attach the borders around the four sides of the quilt and mitre the corners.

QUILTING

Mark diagonal quilting lines over the quilt top, including the border. The lines on this quilt have been drawn so that they follow the diagonals created by the small pieced triangles. The quilting lines are continued across the larger triangles but not the medium ones.

Lay out the backing fabric, pieced to a size slightly larger than the quilt top, and place the wadding and then the pieced quilt on top. Use small safety pins to hold the layers together. Using blending thread and a slightly larger stitch than for normal sewing, quilt the lines you have marked, beginning at a central row and working outwards. Turn the quilt and work on the remaining section. When all the quilting has been completed, remove the pins.

BINDING

Cut seven binding strips 3in wide and join into one long strip. Press in half, wrong sides together, and stitch onto the right side of the quilt. Stop at the corners, ¼in from the edge, and make a mitring fold before stitching the next side. Turn the binding to the wrong side and hand-stitch to cover the machine stitching. Finish by signing your quilt. ❖

Basic Equipment

1	Paper Cutting Scissors	**8**	Needles	**15**	Rotary Cutter
2	Dressmaker's Scissors	**9**	HB Pencil	**16**	100% Cotton Thread
3	Embroidery Scissors	**10**	Silver Marking Pencil	**17**	Cotton/Polyester Thread
4	Tape Measure	**11**	Templates	**18**	Cutting Mat
5	Thimble	**12**	Glass-headed Pins	**19**	Safety Pins
6	Ruby Beholder	**13**	Plastic Ruler		
7	Adjustable Ruler	**14**	Pin Cushion		

BASIC EQUIPMENT

We may have come a long way since quilts were first made in the 1880s, but the basic tools for patchwork such as needles, thread, pins and scissors remain the essentials.

NEEDLES

For machine stitching you will need a supply of new sewing machine needles for light to medium-weight cottons.

A 'betweens' needle is considered the best for both hand piecing and quilting. 'Sharps' are used when a longer needle is required. A good general rule is to use as fine a needle as you can manage comfortably; size 8 is recommended for beginners. If you want to make smaller stitches as you progress, use a smaller needle. Size 12 is the smallest.

THREAD

Traditionally, synthetic threads are used with synthetic fabrics and cotton with cotton fabrics. Polyester-cotton thread (polyester core wrapped in cotton) or 100 per cent cotton thread are best for cotton fabrics and are the easiest to use for all other fabrics. This thread does have a tendency to fray and tangle so avoid this by knotting the end before unrolling the thread, then cutting and threading the other end through the needle.

Select a colour that matches the darkest fabric you are sewing. If you are using different fabrics, select a neutral thread such as grey or ecru which will blend inconspicuously with all of them.

PINS

Glass-headed pins are very sharp and good for piercing straight through the material when lining up a seam or a starting point.

There is a longer pin available which is excellent for pinning together layers on more bulky projects.

SCISSORS

You will need three pairs of scissors for patchwork. Dressmaker's shears, preferably with a bent handle – these should be extremely sharp and used only for cutting fabric. Paper scissors – never cut paper with sewing shears, as this will dull the blades. Embroidery scissors for clipping threads and seam allowances – these should also be very sharp.

ROTARY CUTTER AND MAT

A rotary cutter is an excellent tool for cutting strips, straightening fabric edges and cutting out a variety of geometric patchwork pieces. It also enables more accurate cutting of several layers of fabric at once.

Choose a cutter with a large blade, and keep spare blades handy. Always cut on a mat specially designed for a rotary cutter to keep the blade sharp. Fold the fabric in half on the mat with right sides facing and selvedges matching. The drafting triangle sits directly on the fold of the fabric, the rotary rule sits on the left edge of the triangle. The mat grips the fabric and helps the blade to cut straight. A 'self-healing' cutting mat is ideal.

RULERS

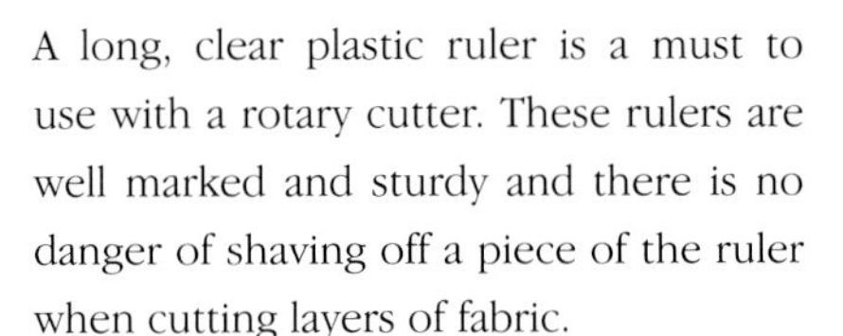

A long, clear plastic ruler is a must to use with a rotary cutter. These rulers are well marked and sturdy and there is no danger of shaving off a piece of the ruler when cutting layers of fabric.

PENCILS

A soft lead pencil is the traditional option for marking a design, but there is also a variety of marking pencils available. Probably the most useful is a water soluble pencil, as it gradually fades after a period of time.

Be careful, however, as the design is liable to disappear before the project can be finished.

TEMPLATES

Templates can be homemade from graph paper, tracing paper and cardboard or template plastic. The edges of cardboard templates tend to wear after frequent cutting of patches, but plastic and metal templates, which are available in a great variety of shapes and sizes, are virtually indestructible. This is a great advantage, especially for a large project which requires cutting out several of each shape.

Window templates are useful if you are featuring or centring a motif or flower in a patch.

Templates for hand sewing, appliqué and quilting are cut to the exact shape without seam allowance. They mark the stitching line not the cutting line. For machine sewing, include 6mm (¼in) seam allowance around all edges.

THIMBLES

A thimble is indispensable if you are quilting by hand. It is also good to use on the finger underneath the work to push the needle back through the fabric.

FRAMES AND HOOPS

A frame or a hoop makes the quilting of large projects, such as bed-sized quilts, much easier. It is not essential to use one for smaller items, but you will get a better finish.

FABRICS

Choosing the most suitable fabric for your patchwork project is important, especially for a beginner. Some fabrics are easier to work with than others. With experience, you will discover which fabric is a joy to use and which is an absolute headache. The most important rules to remember are to buy the best fabric you can afford. A firmly woven, lightweight, 100 per cent pure cotton is easier to use, lasts longer and gives crisp results.

Synthetics and mixtures can be difficult to iron and handle and may pucker along the seams but they are attractive, versatile and can be unusual or striking in appearance. They are often more readily available than 100 per cent cottons, but they are not all easier to use. Some tend to be slippery, floppy and soft.

As you gain experience, you may want to experiment with more exotic fabrics. Many of these will need special handling but to find out about these fabrics, you will have to test them yourself. Some satins and taffeta can be too fragile for patchwork. Synthetics also tend to be more difficult to quilt through as they are slightly spongy.

COLOURS AND PRINTS

The successful combining of colours is often a matter of trial and error, not something that can be taught. The only way to find out if it will work is by trying it.

To achieve a good contrast, you need a mix of prints: small, medium, large, checks, stripes and plains. A mix of colours is also important. Contrast rather than coordinate. You will need a mixture of colour values – twenty per cent darks, forty per cent mediums and forty per cent lights is a good mix.

The value, or the lightness or darkness of a colour, is probably more important than the actual colour when you are making a quilt. To achieve successful results, try to use a range of values.

Many small-scale floral prints are available. Although a safe choice, they are sometimes so safe and well colour-coordinated that they give a rather dull and uninspired finished effect.

Experiment with prints of varying scale, stripes and border designs, geometric prints and checks. Some large-scale prints can introduce a delicate, lacy effect. Take particular care with stripes. If they are not cut and sewn perfectly straight, it will be very obvious.

Certain fabrics are evocative of different eras or styles. Create a country-style quilt by including fabrics which are bold and brightly coloured and include different-sized checks, stripes, ticking, stars and geometric prints.

A 1930s-style quilt can be created by including fabrics such as bright pastels, fresh florals, perky checks, stripes and white backgrounds.

FABRICS TO AVOID

Stretch fabrics such as knits and some crepes should always be avoided. Very closely woven fabrics can also prove difficult, even for machine sewing. This applies to heavy fabrics such as canvas, and lightweight fabrics like some poplins.

Very open weave fabrics can cause difficulties with fraying and because of their transparency.

PREPARATION OF FABRICS

Always wash your fabrics before use. This will pre-shrink them, remove excess dye and remove any sizing, so that the fabric is easier to handle. Machine wash your fabrics unless you have only a small quantity of fabric.

The volume of water used for washing seems to flush the dye and sizing out thoroughly. It is unusual to have a problem such as the dye running from one fabric to others, but if you are not sure of a fabric, always hand wash it separately.

If tumble drying, a short drying time is quite sufficient, unless the pieces are very large.

Don't over-dry fabrics, as they may become very creased. Remove while they are still slightly damp, then iron them.

When you are purchasing batting for your quilt, it is important to read the washing instructions before you make your choice. Some synthetic battings are often unsuitable for ordinary laundering. Always choose natural fibre battings such as wool, cotton or silk. A good mixture is 90 per cent cotton and 10 per cent polyester. This blend is suitable for both hand and machine quilting and it also washes very well. ❆

Basic Instructions

Patchwork quilts can be made in many different ways. Here we give you the basic techniques required to successfully complete a quilt.

DESIGN AND DRAFTING

To adapt a design or border, or see how the quilt will look and fit together, you will need to make a sketch on graph paper.

Graph paper is used for two things – to make small sketches of quilt designs (graph plan) and to make full size drawings of shapes for templates or as guides for rotary cutting.

You can play with different colourings with a graph plan and use it as a reference map as you construct your quilt. This helps to see the relative proportions of the border and quilt and to judge the effect. A sketch also lets you preview your quilt and make improvements before you start cutting and sewing.

A quilt sketch is a drawing of the quilt in miniature. You will need to assign a scale in order to calculate the finished size of the quilt and to draft templates. Keep the scale easy so that cutting dimensions will match standard markings on your rotary cutting ruler.

DRAFTING TEMPLATES

Graph paper marked in ¼in is one of the easiest to use to make full size drawings of template shapes. You can draw a full size block or portion of a border onto graph paper and identify each shape to be cut by lightly colouring it in, then add a consistent ¼in seam allowance around each one. Trace the completed shapes onto template material or use the measurements as cutting guides for template-free rotary cutting.

Template plastic with a ¼in grid is also available, so that shapes can be drawn directly onto it and an accurate seam allowance should be added. If the templates are to be used for machine sewing, add a ¼in seam allowance all around. If the template is being used for hand sewing, add a ¼in seam allowance when cutting out the fabric. Straight grain arrows should be marked onto templates.

Note: The outside edges of a block or quilt must always be on the straight grain, or the quilt will not lie flat. Mark your graphed blocks and borders accordingly.

Glueing a piece of sandpaper to the back of a paper or plastic template, with the gritty side facing down, is a great way of cutting accurate shapes from fabric. The sandpaper adds weight and sturdiness and the rough surface grips the fabric for more accurate cutting.

Note: Do not cut your sandpaper with fabric scissors.

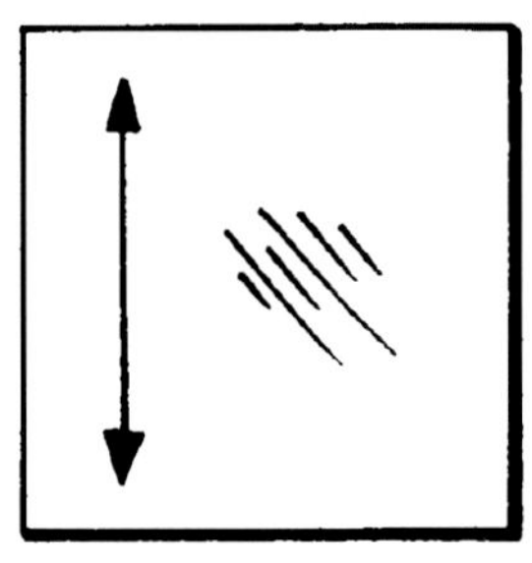

Standard Template

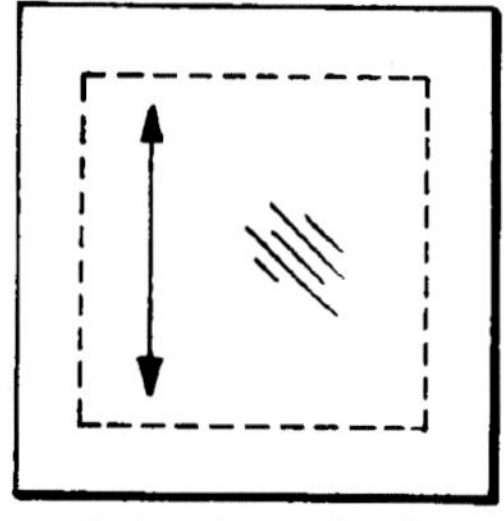

Machine Sewing Template

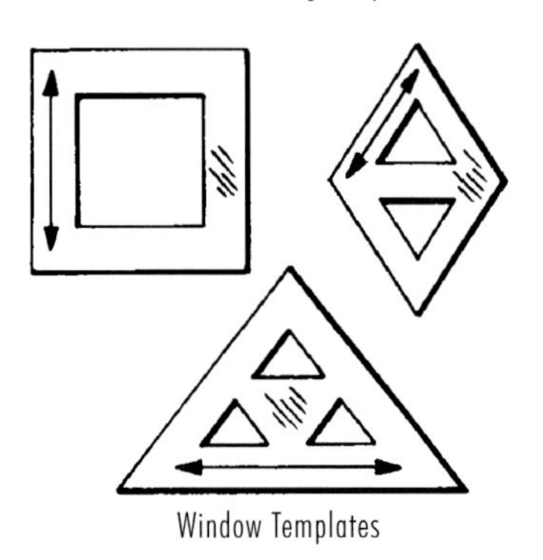

Window Templates

CUTTING

Trim the selvedge from the fabric before you begin. If you are using one fabric for both borders and block pieces, cut the borders first, then the block pieces from what is left over.

Position templates on fabric so that the arrows match the straight grain. With a sharp pencil (an erasable pencil or a white for dark fabrics, or lead pencil for light fabrics), trace around the template on the fabric. Allow a further ¼in all around the drawn shape for seam allowance before cutting out. Templates for machine sewing include a seam allowance, but these pieces must be precisely cut as there is no drawn line to guide your sewing. Multiple layers can be cut at the one time by folding and pressing the fabric into layers before placing the template. Make sure that each piece is cut on the straight grain.

ROTARY OR TEMPLATE-FREE CUTTING

It is important to use the rotary cutter accurately and efficiently to ensure straight pieces. Straighten the fabric by folding it in layers, selvedge to selvedge, to fit on the cutting mat. Lay a triangle along the folded edge of the fabric and push it against the right side of the ruler until it is just at the edge.

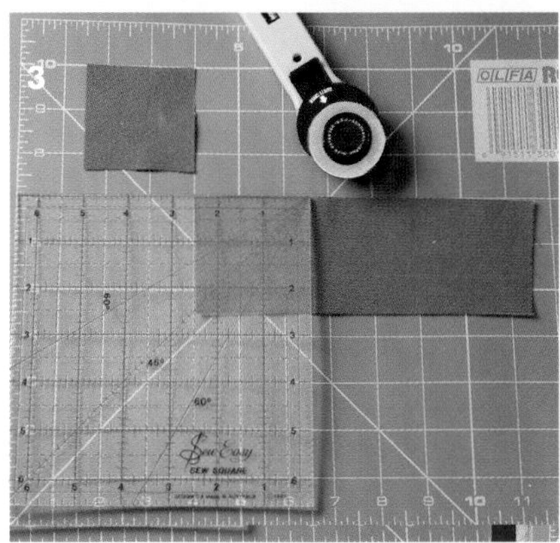

Hold the ruler down with your left hand, remove the triangle and begin cutting. Walk your hand up parallel with the cutter and continue to cut off the end of the fabric. Do not try to hold the ruler at the bottom as you will most likely move it.

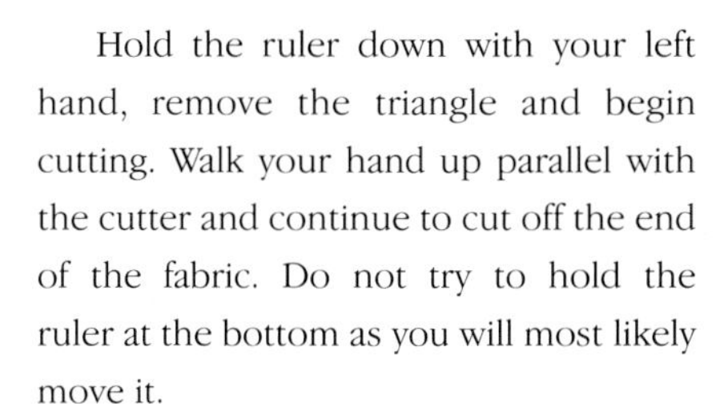

Once you have straightened the fabric, use the cutter and ruler to cut strips of fabric to the width you require.

Squares, rectangles and triangles are all cut from strips. Remember when cutting squares and rectangles to add ½in to the desired finished measurement. For a 2in finished square cut a 2½in square. For a 2in x 4in finished rectangle, cut 2½in x 4½in.

Half square triangles are half a square with the short sides on the straight grain and the long side on the bias. To cut these triangles, cut a square in half diagonally. Cut the square ⅞in larger than the finished short side of the triangle to allow for seam allowances.

Quarter square triangles are used along the outside edge of a quilt

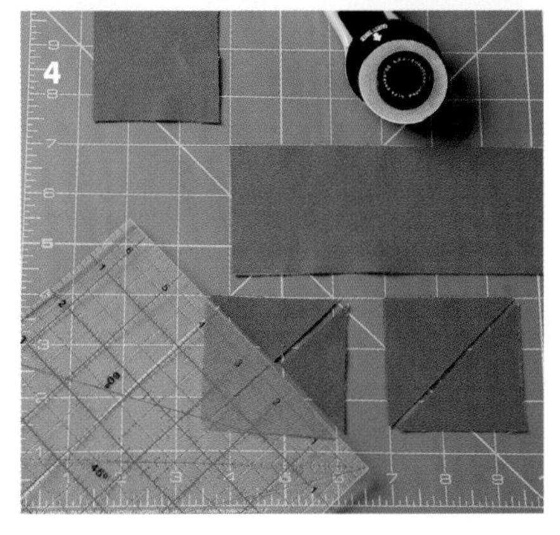

and some blocks are quarter square triangles. These triangles have their short sides on the bias and the long side on the straight grain. These triangles are cut from squares. Each square is cut into four on the diagonal and each is 1¼in larger than the finished long side of the triangle.

PIECING METHODS

Hand Piecing

Pieces for hand piecing require precisely marked seamlines; marked cutting lines are optional.

Place the template face down on the wrong side of the fabric and draw around it accurately with a sharp pencil. Leave space between patches for a ¼in seam allowance when cutting.

After marking the patches, cut outward from the seamline ¼in, measuring the distance by eye. Join the pieces right sides together, so the marked seamline on the wrong side of the fabric is visible on both sides of the patchwork when sewing. Sew the seam through the pencilled lines with a short running stitch and occasional Backstitch, using a single thread.

Begin and end each seam at the seamline (not at the edge of fabric) with two or three Backstitches to secure the seam and sew from point to point, not edge to edge.

When joining the blocks and the rows together, do not sew the seam allowance down. Sew up to the dot marking the corner, then begin on the next side by taking a couple of extra small Backstitches and continue sewing along the line. This leaves your options open as to which way to press the seam allowance when the block is completed.

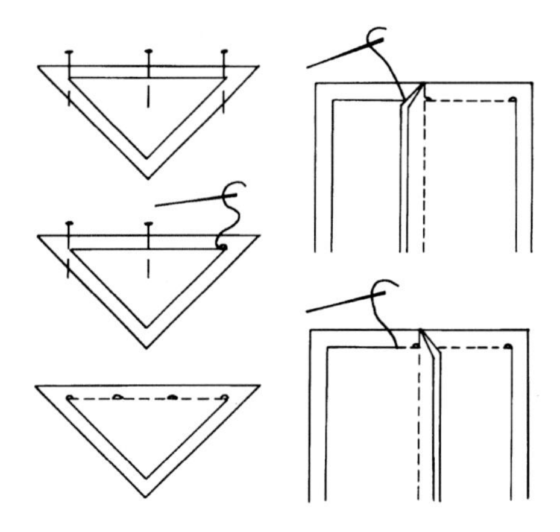

English Paper Piecing Method

This hand piecing technique involves basting fabric over a thin cardboard or paper template. The shapes are stitched together to form blocks and ultimately to form a quilt.

Although time-consuming, this method results in precise, sharp seams and a professionally finished appearance for your project. It also has the advantage of being able to be picked up, put down and carried around so you can work on your project in those spare moments.

Make a master template shape from firm plastic. On gift board, trace the required quantity of each shape. On the wrong side of the selected fabric, trace the required amount of each shape. Cut these out with a generous ¼in seam allowance.

Place the cardboard template in the centre of the wrong side of the fabric shape. Working one side at a time, fold over the seam allowance onto the template. Baste into place through the template, making sure the corners of the fabric are neatly folded in. For easy removal of the basting, start with a knot and finish with a simple double stitch.

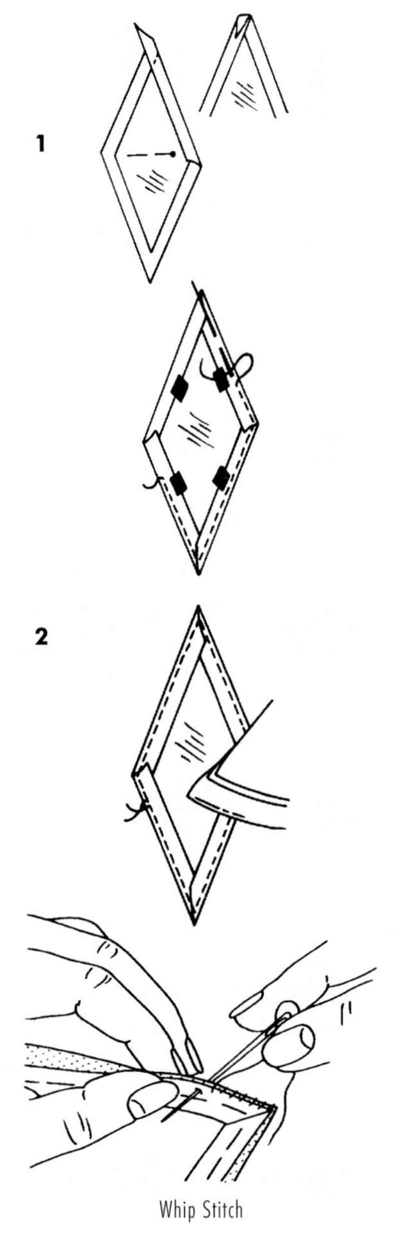

Whip Stitch

To join the patches together, place them right sides facing and match corners. With a matching thread, or a mid-grey thread which blends with most colours, join the edges from corner to corner using a tiny Whipstitch and double stitch the corners. The stitch should be fairly small and not visible from the right side of the fabric.

Make each block separately by sewing the smallest pieces together first to form units. Join smaller units to form larger ones until the block is complete.

Press, then join the blocks together to form rows and the rows together to form the sampler or quilt top.

The cardboard templates can be removed when all the pieces are joined together. Turn the quilt over, press well with a warm iron and allow to cool. Carefully remove the basting stitches and lift out each piece of cardboard separately.

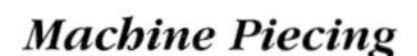

Machine Piecing

Accurate cutting is very important especially in machine piecing. Include seam allowances in the template and mark the cutting line on the back of the fabric.

Use white or neutral thread as light in colour as the lightest colour in the project. Use a dark neutral thread for piecing dark solids.

When machine sewing patches, align cut edges with the edge of the presser foot if it is ¼in wide. If not, place masking tape on the throat plate of the machine ¼in away from the needle to guide you in making ¼in seams. Sew along to the cut edge unless you are inserting a patch into an angle. Short seams need not be pinned unless matching is involved. Keep pins away from the seamline. Sewing over pins is not good for sewing machine needles.

Use chain-piecing whenever it is possible in order to save valuable time and thread. Sew one seam, however do not lift the presser foot. Do not take the piece out of the sewing machine and do not cut the thread.

Instead, you should set up the next piece to be sewn and continue stitching. There will be small twists of thread between the two pieces. Sew all the seams you can at one time, then remove the 'chain'. Clip all of the threads, then press the seams.

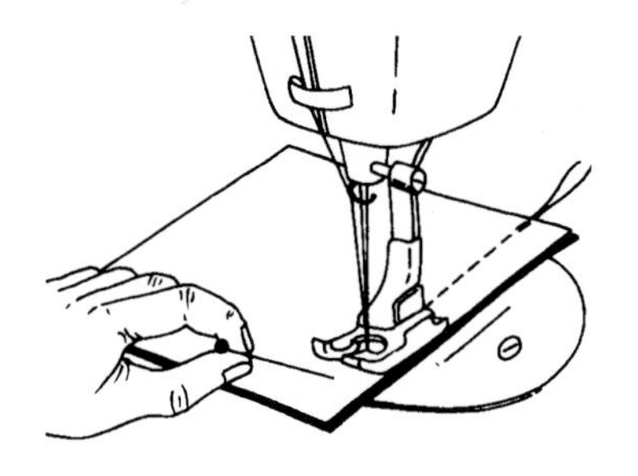

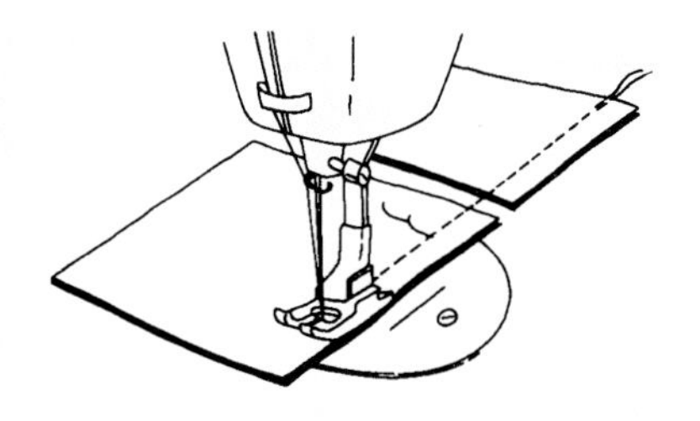

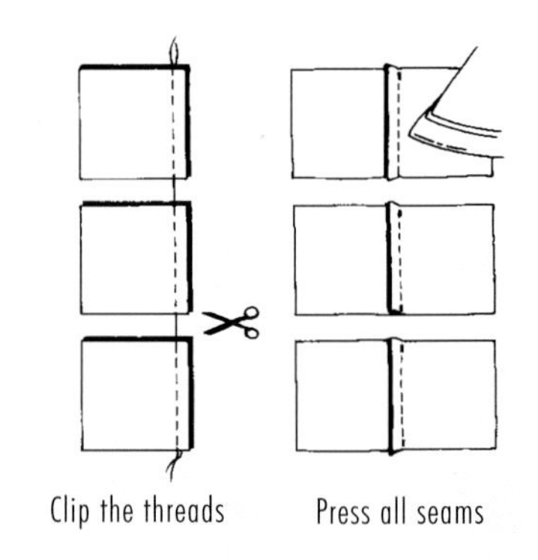
Clip the threads   Press all seams

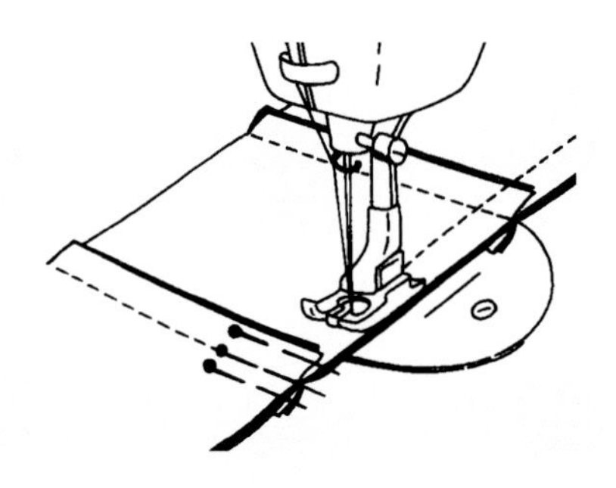

When joining rows, make sure matching seam allowances are pressed in opposite directions to reduce bulk and make matching easier. Pin pieces together directly through stitching and to the right or left of the seam, removing the pins as you sew.

JOINING BLOCKS

Blocks joined edge to edge

Join the blocks to form strips the width of the quilt. Pin each seam very carefully, inserting a pin wherever seams meet, at right angles to the seam using a ¼in seam allowance. Join all blocks in the second row, continuing until all rows are completed. Press all seam allowances in the odd-numbered rows in one direction and all seam allowances in even-numbered rows in the opposite direction. When all rows are completed, pin two rows together so that seamlines match perfectly. Join rows in groups of two, then four, and so on until the top is completed. Press all allowances in one direction, either up or down.

Blocks joined with vertical and horizontal sashing

Join the blocks into strips with a vertical sash between each pair of blocks. Sew a horizontal piece of sashing to each strip, then join the strips to form the quilt top.

PRESSING

Press the seam allowances to one side, usually towards the darker fabric. Press quilt blocks flat and square with no puckers. To correct any problems in blocks, sashes or borders, remove a few stitches to ease puckers and re-sew.

APPLIQUE

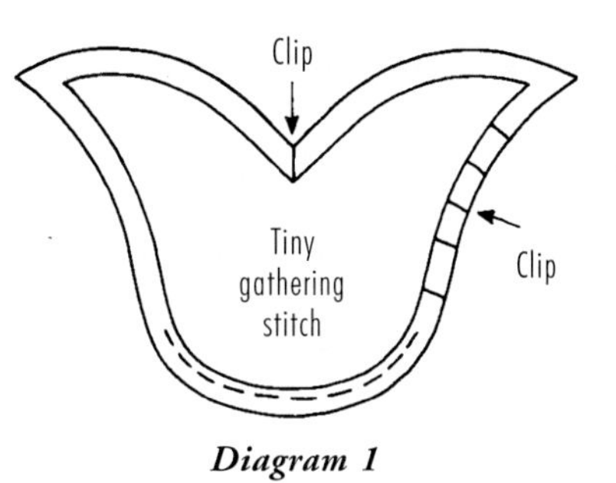

Diagram 1

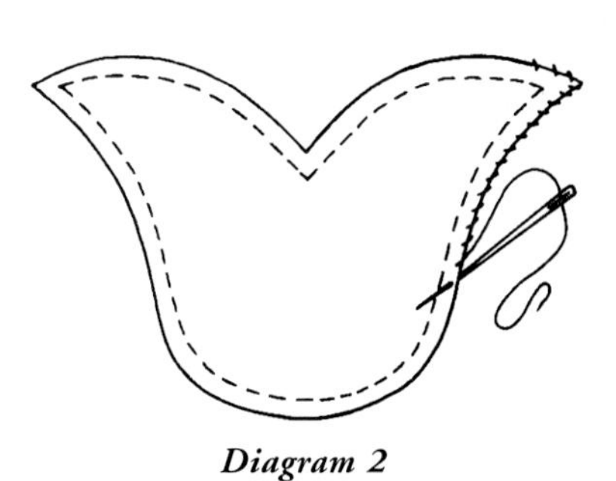

Diagram 2

Appliqué is not a difficult technique but basic rules do apply. Curved shapes should be smooth with no points, points should be a definite point, and there should be no puckers. Begin by marking around the template onto the right side of the fabric. Cut out the shape with a ¼in seam allowance. Turn the seam allowance under and baste. When there is a sharp curve sew a tiny running stitch just to the outside of the marked line. Gather slightly so that the curve sits well (see Diagram 1). Where there is a sharp point, mitre the corner as you are basting, and cut away any excess fabric. Be careful not to cut away too much. Pin the pieces to the background fabric making sure they are centred.

Cut a 15¾in length of thread and make a small knot. Make sure the knot sits underneath the piece being appliquéd, then bring the thread from the back through the background fabric and catch a couple of threads on the appliqué piece. When you begin to appliqué, make sure the needle enters the background fabric directly opposite where it came out on the top piece and slightly under the piece being appliquéd (see Diagram 2). When you have completed stitching, finish off on the back with a couple of small Backstitches.

ADDING MITRED BORDERS

Centre a border strip each side of the quilt top to extend equally at each end. Pin, baste, and sew strips in ¼in seams, beginning and ending at the seamline, not the outer edge of the fabric. At one corner, on the wrong side, smooth one border over the adjacent one and draw a diagonal line from the inner seamline to the point where the outer edges of the two borders cross. Reverse the two borders (the bottom one is now on top), draw a diagonal line from the inner seamline to the point where the outer edges cross. Match the two pencil lines (fabrics right sides together), and sew through them. Cut away the excess, and press the allowances open. Repeat at the other corners of the quilt.

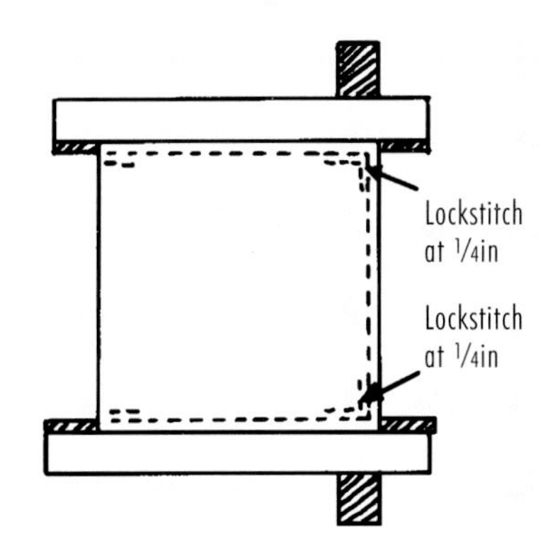

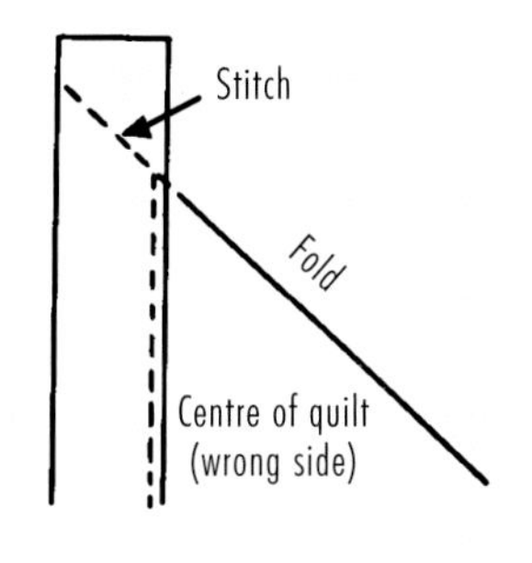

BATTING

Batting is the padding that plumps up the quilt. It goes between the quilt top and the backing. There is a variety of battings on the market, ranging from natural fibres such as cotton and wool to synthetics. Most battings are available in different weights, but a thin, lightweight one is ideal for hand quilting, as it is much easier to produce small, even stitches. A thin batting also gives a more authentic appearance to traditional quilt designs. Thicker battings are useful if you want extra warmth and they can be tied rather than quilted.

BACKING

Make the quilt backing about 2in larger each side than the quilt top. The two or three lengths that need to be sewn must be seamed together. Remove the selvedges to avoid puckers and press the seam allowances open or to one side. Place the backing, wrong side up, on a flat surface. Spread quilt batting over the backing, making sure that both stay smooth and even. Place the quilt top, right side up, on top of the batting. Pin layers as necessary to secure them while basting. Beginning in the centre, baste in an 'X'. Working outwards, baste rows 4in and 6in apart. Baste all around the edges.

MARKING FOR QUILTING

Place a quilting pattern under the quilt top. Lightly mark the design on the top, using a hard lead pencil. Mark dark-coloured fabrics with a chalk pencil. Always test water-soluble pens for removability before marking the quilt. Some quilting may be done without marking the top. Outline quilting ¼in from seam around patches or quilting in the ditch (right next to the seam on the side without the seam allowances) can be done by 'marking' the quilting line by eye. Other straight lines may also be marked as you quilt by using a piece of masking tape that is pulled away after a line is quilted along the edge.

QUILTING

Quilting is done in a short running stitch with a single strand of thread that goes through all three layers. Use a short needle (8 or 9 betweens) with about 18in thread. Make a small knot in the thread and take a first long stitch, about 1in, through the top and batting only, coming up where the quilting will begin. Tug on the thread to pull the knotted end between the layers. Take straight, even stitches that are the same size on the top and bottom of the quilt. For tiny stitches, push the needle with a thimble on your middle finger. Guide the fabric in front of the needle with the thumb of your hand above the quilt and with the thumb and index finger of your other hand below the quilt. To end a line of quilting, take a tiny Back Stitch, make another small knot and pull between the layers. Make another 1in long stitch through the top and batting only and clip the thread at the surface of the quilt. Carefully pull out the basting threads when the quilting is finished.

BINDING

Trim the edges of the quilt. One of the most popular methods of binding is to cut the binding fabric into seven 3in strips, selvedge to selvedge. Join these to make one long strip and press in half along the length, wrong sides together. Sew to the quilt top, starting at the centre bottom, ½in from the raw edges. To mitre the binding, stop ½in from the corner, Backstitch and take out of the machine.

Fold the binding up making a 45 degree angle with the binding strip.

Fold down, level with the edge and sew to the next corner. Repeat and overlap the ends of the binding, Slip Stitch in place to the back of the quilt. A nice finishing touch is to embroider your name, city, and date on the back of the quilt.

CARE OF QUILTS

After spending many hours making a quilt you will want to look after it in the best possible way. Remember, it may well become a future heirloom.

While you obviously want to use and enjoy your quilt, you also want to minimise the amount of wear and tear it receives. Get into the habit of folding back the quilt at night so it lies across the foot of the bed only. Or remove it entirely. In this age of electric blankets and heated waterbeds, a quilt is often decorative rather than functional. If you do need the quilt for warmth at night, place a sheet underneath it.

Turn it back over the top edge of the quilt with at least a metre turn back. This will greatly reduce soiling.

Quilts made from suitable fabrics can be washed successfully, but if you care for your quilt properly, you will reduce the need for frequent washing.

Sunlight weakens the fabric fibres and also fades the colours. If the bed receives direct sunlight it is wise to fold back the quilt or draw the curtains.

STORAGE

Store your quilt by rolling or folding it and wrapping it in an old cotton pillowcase or sheet.

If it is folded, it should be refolded occasionally along different fold lines to avoid permanent creasing.

Never store in a plastic bag as air circulation is essential.

Do not place an unwrapped quilt directly on a wooden shelf as chemicals in the timber can stain the fabric.

WASHING

If possible, hand wash the quilt in a large container such as the bath. Use warm, not hot water and dissolve the detergent before adding the quilt. Soak for 5 to 10 minutes then squeeze gently by hand; do not twist or wring. Rinse thoroughly in lukewarm water. If you want to use fabric conditioner make sure it is stirred into the rinse water and not poured directly onto the quilt.

If you have a washing machine large enough to take the quilt without having to cram it in, spin the quilt to remove excess water, as the excess weight of water can strain the stitching. Use a low speed spin if you have the option.

Dry the quilt outdoors away from direct sunlight. Spread it flat on a clean sheet, or drape it over a patio table. If using the clothesline, spread the quilt over several parallel lines rather than hanging the entire weight of the quilt from one line.

The quilt can be machine washed if you don't have a large enough container. However, do not try to wash a large quilt in a small machine as it cannot be cleaned effectively and the lack of space can damage the quilt. Once the quilt is dry, place it in a tumble dryer on a cool cycle to fluff up the batting.

If the quilt needs to be ironed, place it right side down on a thick towel and steam press gently on the wrong side. ❈

Stitch Guide

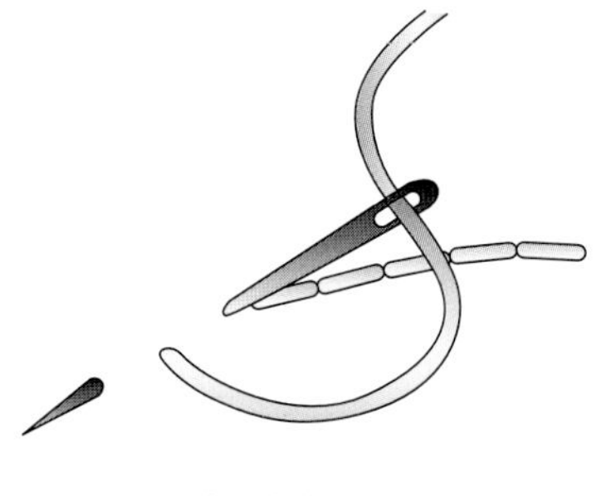

BACK STITCH

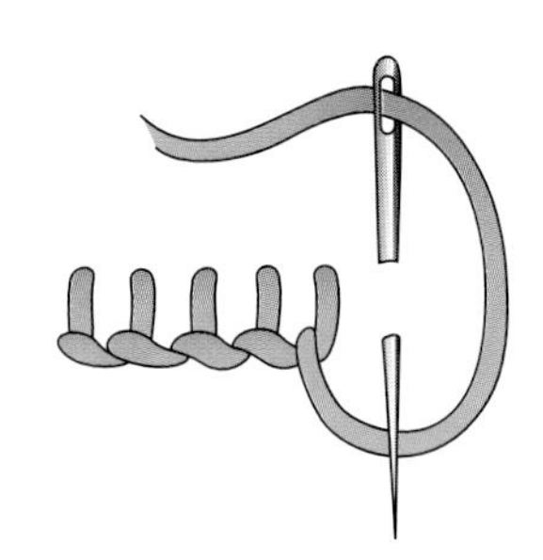

BLANKET STITCH

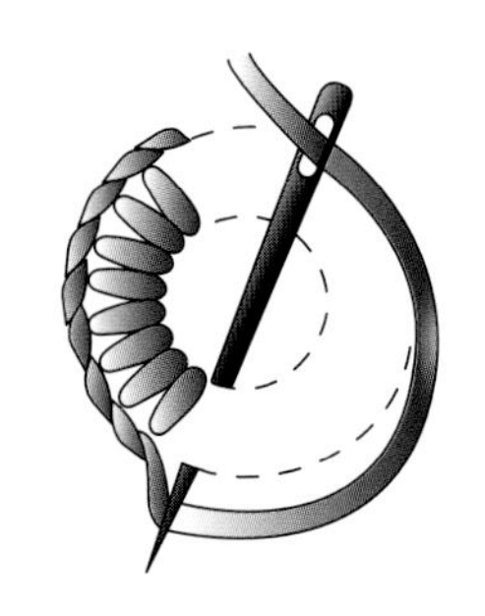

BUTTONHOLE STITCH

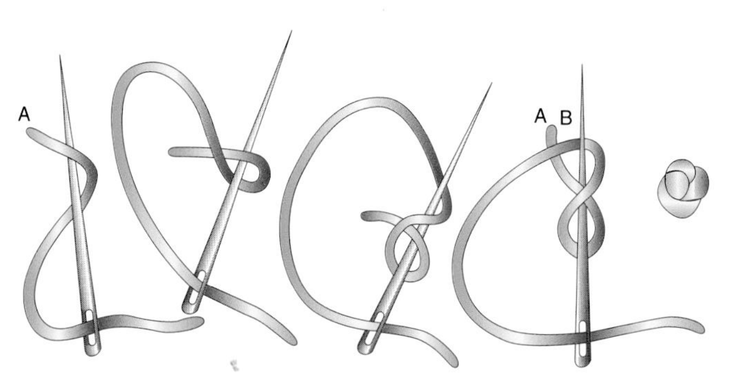

COLONIAL KNOT

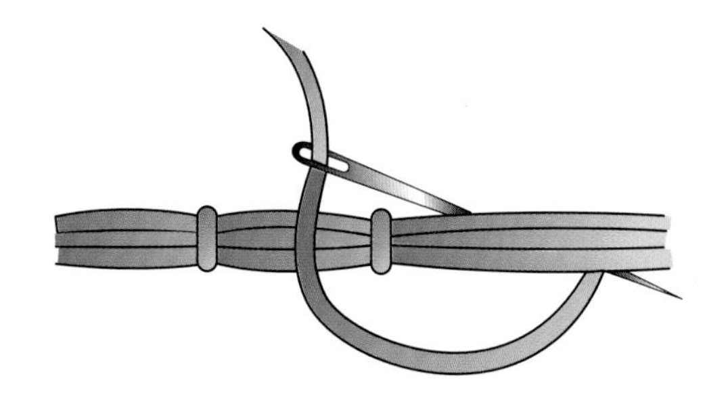

COUCHING

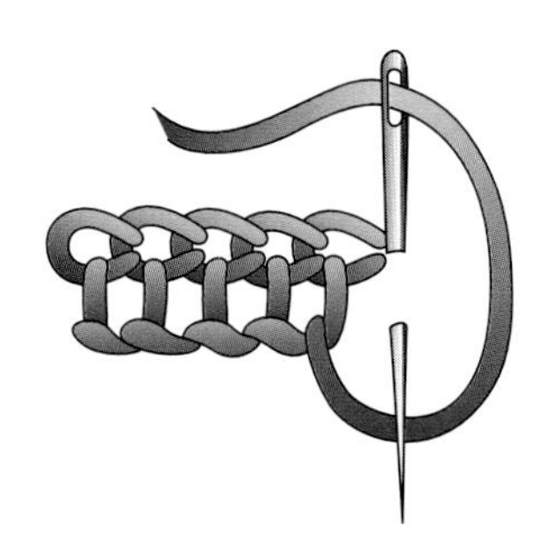

DETACHED BUTTONHOLE STITCH

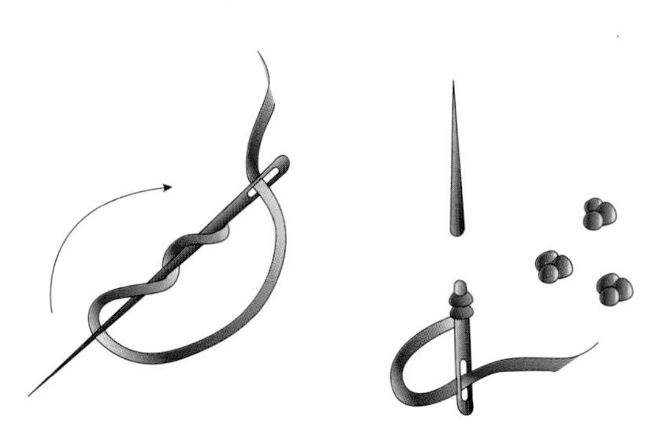

FRENCH KNOT

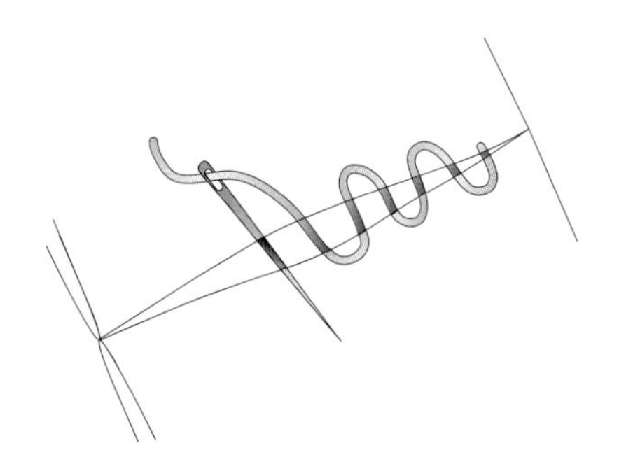

LADDER STITCH

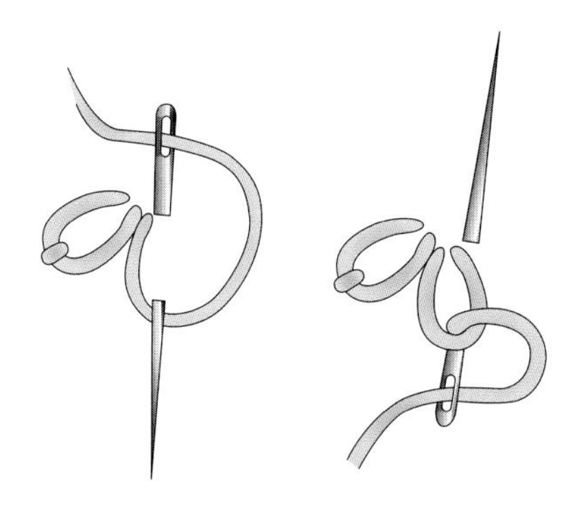
LAZY DAISY STITCH

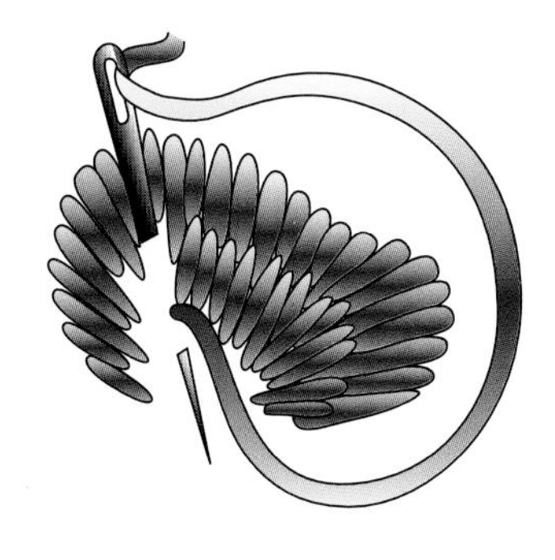
LONG AND SHORT STITCH

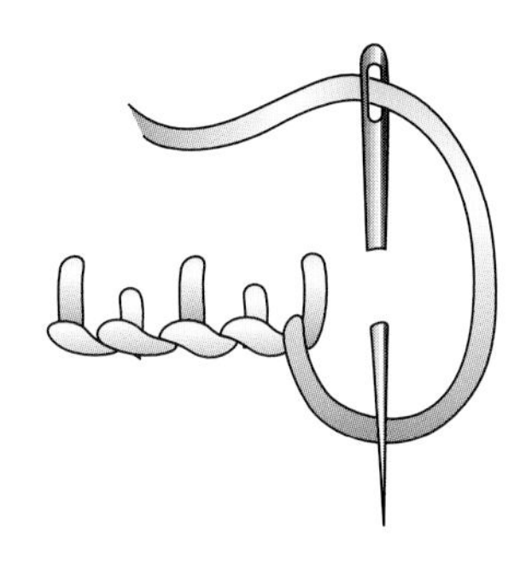
LONG AND SHORT BLANKET STITCH

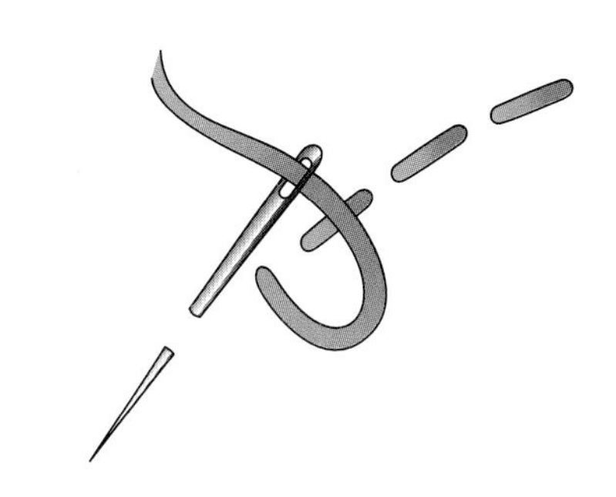
RUNNING STITCH

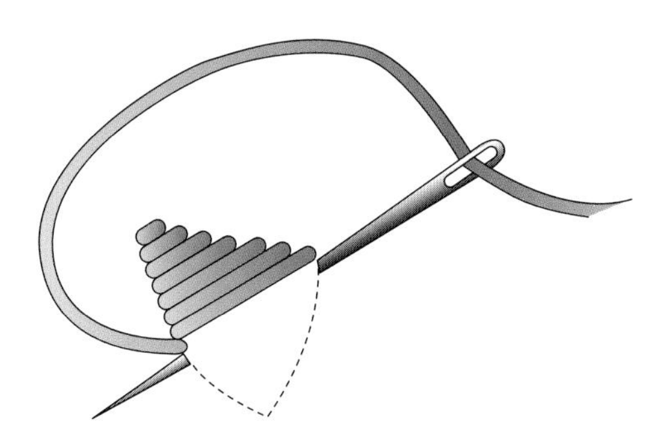
SATIN STITCH

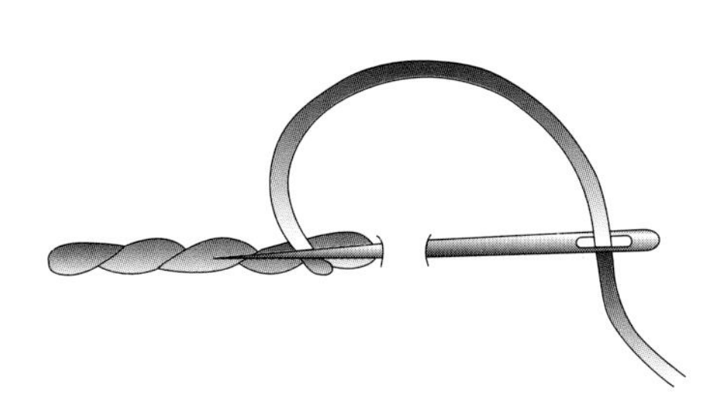
STEM STITCH

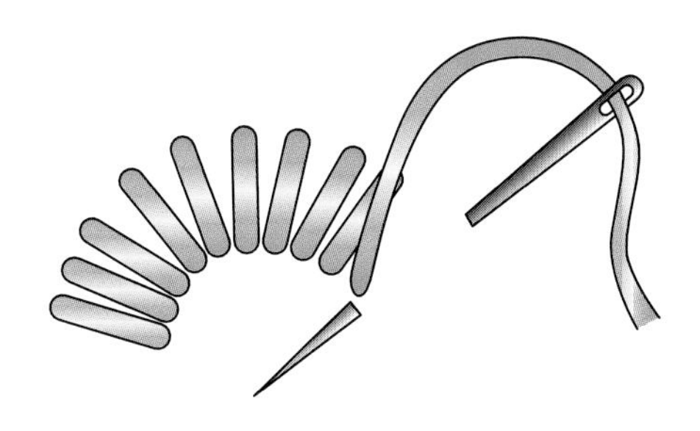
STRAIGHT STITCH

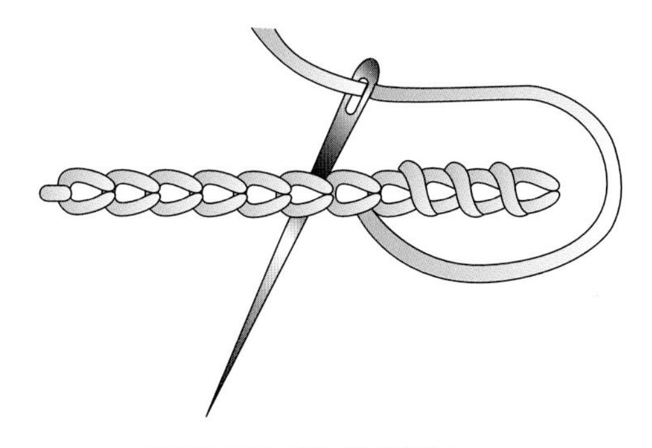
WHIPPED CHAIN STITCH

Index

Note: All project names are in italics

Published by
Craftworld Books
A division of Express Publications Pty Ltd, ACN 057 807 904
Under licence from EP Investments Pty Ltd, ACN 003 109 055 (1995)

2 Stanley Street
Silverwater NSW 2128
Australia

First published by Craftworld Books 1999

Publisher Sue Aiken
Photographic Director Robyn Wilson
Editor Karen Winfield
Production Editors Kylie Davis, Susie Stavens
Designers Jyoti Talwar, Jo Martin

Photographers Tim Connolly, Mark Heriot
Stylists Robyn Wilson, Abbie Mitchell, Peach Panfili, Charlotte Cruise

National Library of Australia Cataloguing-in-Publication data

Fabulous Country-style Quilts

Includes index
ISBN 1875625070

1. Quilting

Printed by KHL Printing Co, Singapore

Australian distribution to supermarkets and newsagents by Network Distribution Company, 54 Park Street, Sydney NSW 2000 Ph (02) 9282 8777.

Overseas Distribution Enquiries Godfrey Vella Ph 61 (2) 9748 0599, Locked Bag 111, Silverwater NSW 1811 Australia
email: gvella@expresspublications.com.au